The
VDM-SL
reference guide

John Dawes

ICL Secure Systems

Pitman

PITMAN PUBLISHING
128 Long Acre, London WC2E 9AN

A Division of Longman Group UK Limited

© J. Dawes 1991

First published in Great Britain 1991

British Library Cataloguing in Publication Data
Dawes, John
　The VDM-SL reference guide.
　I. Title
　005.13
　ISBN 0-273-03151-1

All rights reserved. No part of this publication may be reproduced, stored in a retrieval system, or transmitted, in any form or by any means, electronic, mechanical, photocopying, recording and/or otherwise without either the prior written permission of the Publishers or a licence permitting restricted copying in the United Kingdom issued by the Copyright Licensing Agency Ltd, 90 Tottenham Court Road, London W1P 9HE. This book may not be lent, resold, hired out or otherwise disposed of by way of trade in any form of binding or cover other than that in which it is published, without the prior consent of the publishers.

Printed and bound in Great Britain by
Biddles Ltd, Guildford and King's Lynn

Foreword

This book is offered as an informal guide to the Vienna Development Method Specification Language (VDM-SL) for those who wish to use it without the time or knowledge needed to master the formal definition.

The Vienna Development Method (VDM) is one of the foremost formal methods for the specification and development of systems. One of its main features is the Specification Language (VDM-SL), a mathematically based language for the precise specification of systems. At the time of writing, VDM-SL is undergoing a process of standardization by the British Standards Institution. This process, as with most language standardization efforts, seeks to reconcile the different dialects that have developed. It is also producing a formal, mathematically sound, semantics for the language, which will need a certain degree of mathematical knowledge to master. Designers of computer-based tools for manipulating VDM-SL will of course need this knowledge; but those who simply wish to use VDM-SL to gain increased precision and confidence do not, and it is for them that this book has been written.

The standardization process has now reached a stage where the main features of the language are stable, but some details are still liable to change. This book is based on the latest draft of the Standard; it will not be invalidated to any but a minor degree by the final Standard, but there will probably be some changes of detail. For example, the presentation of the concrete syntax is at present under review, including the names of constructs, but any changes made are unlikely to change the actual language to any great degree. Of course the Standard will be the only authoritative definition of VDM-SL.

I would like to thank my colleagues at ICL and on the BSI VDM-SL Standardization Panel who have read early drafts of the book and made many valuable and constructive comments. In particular, my thanks go to Mike Anderson of ICL and to Graeme Parkin and Nicola Bellingham of the National Physical Laboratory.

Contents

1 INTRODUCTION
1.1 Introduction to the book ... 1
1.2 Outline of VDM-SL ... 2
1.3 A short example of VDM-SL ... 4
1.4 Use of identifiers (scope rules) ... 5
1.5 Type constraints ... 6
1.6 Proof obligations ... 7
1.7 Notation ... 8

2 LEXICAL STRUCTURE
2.1 Layout rules ... 11
2.2 Character set ... 12
2.3 Symbols ... 14
2.4 Comments ... 18

3 OVERALL STRUCTURE
3.1 Documents and definitions ... 19
3.2 Types and type definitions ... 20
3.3 Values and value definitions ... 24
3.4 The state ... 25

4 BASIC AND QUOTE TYPES
4.1 General ... 29
4.2 Boolean values ... 31
4.3 Numeric values ... 35
4.4 Characters ... 42
4.5 Quote types ... 44

5 COMPOUND TYPES
5.1 General ... 45
5.2 Sets ... 48
5.3 Maps ... 55
5.4 Sequences ... 65
5.5 Composite values (records) ... 72
5.6 Product values (tuples) ... 78
5.7 Union and optional types ... 81
5.8 Function values ... 84

Contents

6 EXPRESSIONS
- 6.1 General — 89
- 6.2 Patterns and binds — 92
- 6.3 Unary and binary expressions — 97
- 6.4 Complex expressions — 102
- 6.5 Composite expressions — 105
- 6.6 Quantified and iota expressions — 109

7 FUNCTIONS
- 7.1 Function definitions — 115
- 7.2 Implicit function definitions — 117
- 7.3 Explicit function definitions — 121
- 7.4 Curried functions — 124
- 7.5 Polymorphic function definitions — 127

8 OPERATIONS
- 8.1 Operation definitions — 131
- 8.2 Implicit operation definitions — 133
- 8.3 Explicit operation definitions — 139
- 8.4 Operation calls — 141

9 STATEMENTS
- 9.1 General — 143
- 9.2 Commands and bind preambles — 145
- 9.3 Handlers — 151
- 9.4 Assign commands — 156
- 9.5 Nondeterministic commands — 158
- 9.6 Loops — 160
- 9.7 Conditional commands — 164

10 MODULES
- 10.1 Module interfaces and bodies — 167
- 10.2 Import and export — 170
- 10.3 Parameterized modules — 173
- 10.4 Names — 179

Appendix A Collected Mathematical Syntax — 181

Appendix B ISO 646 Syntax — 195

Appendix C Examples of VDM-SL Specifications — 203

Index — 213

List of Tables

Table 1	Informal syntactic notation	9
Table 2	Graphic characters	13
Table 3	Symbolic literals	16
Table 4	Implicitly declared identifiers	17
Table 5	Keywords and compound delimiters	17
Table 6	Basic and quote types	30
Table 7	Logical operators	34
Table 8	Truth tables for the logical operators	34
Table 9	Numeric operations	41
Table 10	Values of rem, div, and mod	41
Table 11	Compound type expressions	47
Table 12	Set operators and expressions	54
Table 13	Map operators and expressions: map operators	63
Table 14	Map operators and expressions: map constructors and applications	64
Table 15	Sequence operators and expressions	71
Table 16	Composite value operators and expressions	77
Table 17	Tuple operators and expressions	80
Table 18	Function operators and expressions	87
Table 19	Patterns	96
Table 20	Unary operators — summary	100
Table 21	Binary operators — summary	101
Table 22	Complex expressions	104
Table 23	Composite expressions	108
Table 24	Quantified and iota expressions	113
Table 25	ISO 646 syntax — character set	199
Table 26	Keywords in the ISO 646 syntax	200
Table 27	ISO 646 syntax summary	201

1 Introduction

1.1 Introduction to the book

The basis of the definition of VDM-SL is the *abstract syntax,* which exhibits the structure of the language at an abstract level, with details of the concrete representation stripped away. The definition of the language in terms of a physical representation, for example as sequences of characters, is by a *concrete syntax*. The draft Standard defines two particular concrete syntaxes. In this book the *mathematical syntax* is used for the language definition; this syntax is intended primarily for publication. The *ISO 646 syntax*, which is intended primarily for electronic information exchange, is described in Appendix B.

Each of the 9 following chapters concerns an aspect of the language, and is divided into sections on particular language features. Each section in general contains the following subsections.

- *Syntax.* This subsection contains the relevant parts of the mathematical syntax, as given in the draft Standard. For a description of the notation used, see Appendix A. This is the most stable part of the language, and little or no change is to be expected in the final Standard, except perhaps for the details of the productions and the construct names.

- *Meaning* This subsection gives an informal description of the meaning of the syntactic constructs, based on the dynamic semantic definition of the draft Standard. This is still under review at the time of writing, and some changes are possible. It is unlikely that any such changes will affect the straightforward use of VDM-SL in the majority of cases, as they will mostly be caused by difficulties in the mathematical definition of obscure cases. This subsection also gives the scope of any declarations, and any type constraints on constituent constructs.

- *Examples.* Some examples are given, chosen to illustrate important points concerning the use of the language features. Sometimes advice on usage is offered, which of course the reader is free to accept or to reject.

1.2 Outline of VDM-SL

VDM-SL is a language for specification as well as development. This entails one of its main characteristics in which it differs from programming languages: a VDM-SL specification is in general *loosely specified* – it does not define a single entity, but rather a class of entities, any one of which satisfies the specification. In the formal semantics these are called *models* of the specification; in practical terms they can be thought of as possible implementations of the specification. This looseness pervades the language, so that in general the meaning of a construct such as a function definition is not a single function but a set of functions.

The main components of a VDM-SL specification are: type definitions, value definitions, function definitions, operation definitions, and a state definition.

Type definitions define the types of the values defined in the specification. A *type* is a set of values, distinguished by the operations that can be performed on them. VDM-SL has a set of basic types such as integers and characters, and a rich repertoire of type constructors by which new types (sets, lists, records, and so on) can be created. In particular, a type can be created from an existing type by imposing an *invariant*, a condition which values of the new type must satisfy. Types (including invariants) may not be loosely specified.

Value definitions define fixed values to be used in the specification; they are similar to parameterless function definitions.

Function definitions define *functions*, which are rules for deriving values (the *results*) from other values (the *parameters*). A function can be defined explicitly by giving an expression for the result, or implicitly by giving a *postcondition* which the result must satisfy. In either case, a function may be loosely specified; this is interpreted as meaning that it specifies a family of functions, any of which would satisfy the specification, but one particular function from the family must be chosen, and then the result is well defined. This form of looseness is called *underspecification*.

Operation definitions define *operations*; these are like functions but are allowed to retain a history of their invocations. A function always returns the same result for the same parameters, but an operation need not. The record of the history is called the *state*, and is defined by the state definition; this has the form of a set of variable declarations which are read and written by the operations. Operations are defined either explicitly, by giving an algorithm for deriving the effect (the result and any changes to the state), or implicitly by giving a postcondition.

Like functions, operations can be loosely specified, but the interpretation is different; a loosely specified operation allows an implementation to return any of the values (not necessarily the same one for every call). This form of looseness is called *nondeterminism*.

VDM-SL provides a means to structure large specifications into more or less self-contained units called *modules*. The module structuring features are almost independent of the rest of the language (called the *flat language*). Facilities are provided for importing types, values, functions, and operations from other modules, and also for writing parameterized modules and instantiating them with specific values for the parameters (which can be types, values, functions, and operations).

VDM-SL contains a variety of operators and other constructs for creating expressions. It also includes *statements*; these are like statements in a programming language, and are used only in the explicit definition of operations.

1.3   A short example of VDM-SL

The following short example of VDM-SL is intended to give the flavour of the language. It is a very abstract specification of a drink vending machine, offering an unspecified variety of drinks: the customer inserts at least the correct money, chooses a drink, and collects the chosen drink and the change. The example is elaborated further in the book.

types
    $Drink$ = **token**   -- an unspecified type
    $Money$ = $\mathbb{N}$ -- a whole number (of pence)

state $Vending\text{-}Machine\text{-}1$ **of**
    $BALANCE : Money$ -- money held by the machine during a transaction
    $PRICES : Drink \xrightarrow{m} Money$ -- the price of each type of drink
  inv $mk\text{-}Vending\text{-}Machine\text{-}1(-, c) \triangleq \forall d : Drink \cdot d \in \mathbf{dom}\ c$
    -- every drink always has a price; c stands for $PRICES$
  init $mk\text{-}Vending\text{-}Machine\text{-}1(c, -) \triangleq c = 0$
    -- initial state: no money in the machine; c stands for $BALANCE$

operations
    $INSERT\text{-}MONEY(cash : Money)$ -- customer inserts some money
    ext wr $BALANCE : Money$ -- this operation can alter the balance
    post $BALANCE = \overleftarrow{BALANCE} + cash$
      -- the operation adds the inserted money to the balance

    $GET\text{-}DRINK(choice : Drink)$ return : $Drink \times Money$
      -- customer chooses drink and gets drink and change
    ext wr $BALANCE : Money$
        rd $PRICES : Drink \xrightarrow{m} Money$ -- this operation can alter
          -- the balance and read (but not alter) the price table
    pre $BALANCE \geq PRICES(choice)$ -- the operation is defined only if
        -- the balance is enough to pay for the chosen drink
    post $(BALANCE = 0) \wedge$
        $(return = mk\text{-}(choice, \overleftarrow{BALANCE} - PRICES(choice)))$
      -- the effect is to clear the balance and to deliver the chosen drink
      -- and the change

1.4 Use of identifiers (scope rules)

The rules for the use of identifiers can be explained in terms of scope rules, as for block-structured programming languages such as Algol 60 and its descendants.

Every identifier in a VDM-SL specification is introduced at a specific occurrence, which may be called its *declaration*. The declaration also associates the identifier with an entity: a value, function, variable, and so on. This association holds over a region of VDM-SL text called the *scope* of the declaration, within which (with exceptions noted below) any use of the identifier denotes the associated entity. In certain cases an identifier may be reused within the scope of one declaration to denote a different entity, by a declaration with a nested scope. Within the inner scope, the outer declaration is hidden. VDM-SL also allows identifiers in certain cases to be used to denote more than one entity within the same scope; in these cases the different uses are syntactically distinguishable.

In the flat language, the scope of many declarations is the entire specification; such declarations are said to have *global scope*. In the structured language described in chapter 10, global scope is confined to a single module; special features are provided for accessing entities across modules.

Recursive function and operation calls can lead to multiple copies of a variable or a value being in existence at the same time. This does not affect the scope rules, as only one copy is visible within one invocation of the function or operation; the situation is exactly the same as in a block-structured programming language.

As an example of the application of the scope rules, consider the vending machine specification in section 1.3. The declarations of *Drink*, *Money*, *BALANCE*, and *PRICES* all have global scope; but the scope of the declaration of *c* in the invariant definition:

$$\textbf{inv } mk\text{-}Vending\text{-}Machine\text{-}1(-, c) \triangleq \forall d : Drink \cdot d \in \textbf{dom } c$$

is just the body of the invariant definition after $\triangleq$. This allows *c* to be declared in the initialization, and would hide an outer declaration of *c*.

1.5 Type constraints

VDM-SL provides a number of *basic types* and a number of ways of defining new types, of three main kinds. There are several *type constructors* for defining types of sets, lists, and so on, with components from other types. A type may be defined by restricting the members of another type by means of an *invariant*. Finally, a type can be defined as the *union* of two or more types, so that it contains all the members of all the component types.

From this it can be seen that VDM-SL is not in general a strongly typed language in the usual sense; it is not possible to assign each expression and each context a unique type and to define type rules on that basis. Instead, rules can be given as to the possible values in general of each form of expression and the acceptable values for each context; in many cases these can be expressed in terms of the type structure but in others they depend on the possible values of components of the expression. For example, for the division i/j to be defined requires i and j to belong to $\mathbb{R}$, the type of real numbers; but it also requires j to be nonzero, which may be implied by the type of j but may need to be proved. Even the fact that i and j are real numbers may need to be proved if they are defined to be of a union type. If the conditions do not hold, the expression is said to have an *undefined value*, or to be undefined. Variables however have well defined types, and any value assigned to a variable must belong to the variable's type: see section 9.4.

The shielding effect of certain structures against undefined values further weakens the type rules by allowing undefined expressions, including ill-typed expressions, in certain contexts. For instance, although the operands of the operator + must be numeric for the result to be defined, the conditional expression:

if true then 3 **else false** + "*ABC*"

is valid, being a well-typed though overelaborate way of writing 3.

1.6 Proof obligations

The term *proof obligation* generally refers to the aspects of the well-formedness of a specification that cannot easily be statically checked. The type rules give rise to proof obligations in certain situations, as noted above. This is one aspect of the general proof obligation of *implementability*, that it is possible to have a system that satisfies the specification. Another example is the obligation to show for each implicitly defined operation that for any set of parameters of the correct types that satisfy the precondition, there is a value of the result type that satisfies the postcondition. For example, take the operation *GET-DRINK* of section 1.3. This returns a result, the second component of which is of type *Money*, which is $\mathbb{N}$, the natural numbers 0, 1, 2, etc. The postcondition ensures only that this component is an integer (since it is the difference between two integers); there is a proof obligation to show that, assuming that the precondition holds, there is a value of the component satisfying the postcondition which is non-negative. If this were not the case, then the operation would be unimplementable.

Another example is that in general an expression must have a defined value for all possible values of its operands; thus if the expression $1/x$ is used, it is necessary to show that x is not 0. This can be shown if the expression is shielded by a suitable condition, as in the conditional expression:

if $x \neq 0$ **then** $1/x$ **else** 1

VDM-SL also allows the Boolean expressions such as the following (see section 4.2):

$(x \neq 0) \land (1/x \neq 1)$

Cases where expression operands are allowed to have undefined values are noted in the appropriate places; in all other cases for an expression to be defined it can be assumed that all its operands must be defined.

There is no hard and fast distinction between static constraints and proof obligations; accordingly all constraints are described together in the subsection *Meaning*.

1.7　Notation

In order to explain the meanings of constructs without constant repetition of the construct names used in the syntax, an *informal syntactic notation* is used in which 1-letter and 2-letter symbols, sometimes decorated with subscripts and/or primes, stand for constructs of various kinds. The usage is consistent, and summarized in Table 1, though reference to Table 1 should not be necessary as the names used are always defined. The symbols are also used in the description to mean the entities denoted by the corresponding syntactic construct; thus 'the type T' is used for 'the type denoted by the type expression T'. It is hoped this will cause no confusion.

The summary tables of expressions indicate the type constraints by signatures of the form $T_1 \times T_2 \times ... \times T_n \rightarrow T$, where the T_i and T are type expressions. This is intended to indicate that each constituent operand or pattern (but not bind) must be of the kind of type shown by the corresponding T_i, and that if so the result is of type T. For instance, for a sequence comprehension (see Table 15):

$[E \mid Id \in S \cdot B]$

the signature given is $T \times \mathbb{R}\text{-set} \times \mathbb{B} \rightarrow T^*$. This means that E can have any value, S must be a set of real numbers, and B must be a Boolean value; and that if T is any type containing the values of E, then the value of the expression is a member of sequence type T^*.

In one further abuse of notation, the form $E_1 = E_2$ is used to mean that either the expressions E_1 and E_2 have the same value, or they are both undefined; and similarly for $E_1 \neq E_2$, $E_1 < E_2$, $E_1 \Leftrightarrow E_2$, and so on.

1.7 Introduction – Notation

Table 1 Informal syntactic notation

symbol	meaning	section
@Id	type variable	7.5
B	Boolean expression	4.2
Bd	bind	6.2
E	general expression	6.1
F	function expression or name	5.8, 7.1
Fd	field	3.4, 5.5
Id	general identifier	2.3
M	map expression	5.3
Md	mode	8.2
Ms	module signature	10.1
N	non-negative integer expression	4.3
Nm	general name	10.4
Op	operation name	8.1
Pt	pattern	6.2
Pb	pattern or bind	6.2
Q	sequence expression	5.4
R	record expression or name	5.5
S	set expression	5.2
Sd	state designator	9.4
St	statement	9.1
T	general type expression	3.2
Tu	tuple expression	5.6
X	numeric expression	4.3
Z	integer expression	4.3

2 Lexical Structure

The *lexical structure* is concerned with how a VDM-SL text is divided into a sequence of *symbols*, the basic syntactic units. The syntax rules in this chapter are at a different level from those in the rest of the book; they give the rules for forming symbols as sequences of characters, rather than for forming language constructs as sequences of symbols. The practical difference is that for the rules in this chapter no separators (spaces and newlines) are allowed between consecutive items.

2.1 Layout rules

As the mathematical syntax is intended primarily for written and printed media, the layout of the text is not rigorously defined. White space and line break are used as separators of adjacent symbols when required, so that any amount of adjacent white space, possibly plus a line break, is regarded as forming a notional *separator*. The distinction between a separator containing a line break (called *newline*) and one without (called *space*) is significant only for terminating a comment — see section 2.4. Apart from this such matters as blank lines, indentation, and pagination have no significance in the language (but can and should be used to improve readability). It is also allowed to intersperse VDM-SL text with other material (for example natural language text) in any way that allows the two to be unambiguously distinguished.

2.2 Character set

2.2.1 Syntax

character = letter | digit | delimiter character | other character
 | separator;

letter = plain letter | keyword letter | distinguished letter
 | Greek letter;

separator = space | newline;

2.2.2 Meaning

At the lowest formal level, a VDM-SL text is a sequence of *characters*. Characters are used to form symbols and have no individual meaning. The character set for the mathematical syntax contains the following (see Table 2); characters other than separators are called *graphic characters*:

- four distinct sets of *letters* (two with both upper and lower case letters, and two with one case only);

- the decimal *digits*;

- a set of *delimiter characters* which form symbols (called simple delimiters) by themselves;

- a number of *other characters* which are used only to form multicharacter symbols;

- the notional *separators* space and newline, derived from the layout as described in section 2.1.

The typeface used has no significance in general. The only exception is that as all the different characters must be distinguishable, certain distinctions must be preserved, though the actual differences of typeface used to make the distinction is undefined (it could for instance be by size, relative position, fount, or style). The conventions adopted in this book are shown in Table 2; slightly different conventions are used in the draft Standard to conform to a different typographical style.

Plain and Greek letters are used to form *identifiers*. Keyword letters are used to form *keywords*. Distinguished letters are used to form *quote literals* (the VDM-SL term for enumeration literals). Digits are used to form *numeric literals* and identifiers.

2.2 Lexical Structure – Character set

Table 2 Graphic characters

plain letters

a b c d e f g h i j k l m n o p q r s t u v w x y z
A B C D E F G H I J K L M N O P Q R S T U V W X Y Z

keyword letters

a b c d e f g h i j k l m n o p q r s t u v w x y z

distinguished letters

A B C D E F G H I J K L M N O P Q R S T U V W X Y Z

Greek letters

α β γ δ ε ζ η θ ι κ λ μ ν ξ ο π ρ σ τ υ φ χ ψ ω
Α Β Γ Δ Ε Ζ Η Θ Ι Κ Λ Μ Ν Ξ Ο Π Ρ Σ Τ Υ Φ Χ Ψ Ω

digits

0 1 2 3 4 5 6 7 8 9

delimiter characters (forming simple delimiters)

, ; : . ( ) [ ] { } + − × / ↑
= ≠ < > ≤ ≥ ¬ ∧ ∨ ⇒ ⇔ ∀ ∃ | ·
∈ ∉ ∩ ∪ ⊂ ⊆ ⋂ ⋃ ↦ ▷ ◁ ▶ ◀ -1 ∘
~ ι λ μ * + $\overset{m}{\leftrightarrow}$ $\overset{m}{\rightarrow}$ $\mathcal{F}$ 𝔹 ℕ ℕ₁ ℤ ℚ ℝ
≙ ∥ → $\overset{o}{\rightarrow}$ ` † ↩

other characters (used only to form multicharacter symbols)

' " - @ !

2.3 Lexical Structure – Symbols

2.3 Symbols

2.3.1 Syntax

   symbol = delimiter | identifier | type variable identifier
      | basic type membership identifier | symbolic literal;

   delimiter = keyword | delimiter character | compound delimiter;

   identifier = (plain letter | Greek letter),
      {plain letter | Greek letter | digit | " ' " | ' - '};

   type variable identifier = '@', identifier;

   basic type membership identifier =
      'is-', ('B' | 'N$_1$' | 'N' | 'Z' | 'Q' | 'R' | 'char' | 'token');

   symbolic literal = boolean literal | numeric literal | character literal
      | text literal | quote literal | nil literal;

   boolean literal = **'true'** | **'false'**;

   numeric literal = numeral, ['.', digit, {digit}], [exponent];

   numeral = digit, {digit};
   exponent = '×10↑', ['+' | '–'], numeral;

   character literal = " ' ", character – separator, " ' ";

   text literal = ' " ', {' "" ' | character – (' " ' | separator)}, ' " ';

   quote literal = distinguished letter, {'-' | distinguished letter};

   nil literal = **'nil'**;

2.3.2 Meaning

Symbols are the smallest meaningful units of the VDM-SL language. They are of 5 kinds: *delimiters, identifiers, type variable identifiers, basic type membership identifiers,* and *symbolic literals.*

No separators are allowed within a symbol. Where necessary to prevent ambiguity, separators are required between adjoining symbols, though this is rarely necessary in practice.

Identifiers are used as names of entities of many kinds. The most general form is a sequence of plain or Greek letters, digits, hyphens, and primes, starting with a letter. The other forms are specialized: a *type variable*

2.3 Lexical Structure – Symbols

identifier is used to denote a type variable in a polymorphic function definition (see section 7.5); and a *basic type membership identifier* is used in a *type membership expression* to test a value for membership of a basic type (see section 3.2). As a rule, identifiers are explicitly declared in the VDM-SL text. There are no predefined identifiers, but some identifiers are implicitly declared; they are derived from explicitly declared identifiers and have associated meanings; see Table 4. Because of its use in tuple constructions (section 5.6) and tuple patterns (section 6.2), *mk-* cannot be used as an identifier.

Symbolic literals are used to denote fixed values. The different kinds of symbolic literals are described in the sections of chapter 4, according to type; Table 3 gives an overview of what is available.

Delimiters have fixed meanings defined implicitly by the meanings of the constructs in which they occur. They comprise the keywords (see Table 5) and special symbols consisting of 1 or more other graphic characters. A special symbol consisting of a single graphic character is called a *simple delimiter* (see Table 2); one consisting of two or more is called a *compound delimiter* (see Table 5). No separator is allowed within a compound special symbol.

2.3.3 Examples

In the VDM-SL specification of section 1.3, the following symbols occur.

Identifiers:	Drink	Money	Vending-Machine-1	BALANCE
	PRICES	mk-Vending-Machine-1	c	d
	INSERT-MONEY	cash	GET-DRINK	choice
	return			

symbolic literals: 0

keywords:	types	token	state	of
	dom	inv	init	operations
	ext	wr	post	rd
	pre			

delimiters:	=	$\mathbb{N}$	:	--	$\xrightarrow{m}$	(	-
	,	)	$\triangleq$	$\forall$	.	$\in$	$\leftharpoonup$
	+	×	$\geq$	$\wedge$	mk-		

The rules for forming identifiers are very free, but the intended usage is that an identifier is a single Greek letter or a sequence of plain letters,

15

2.3 Lexical Structure – Symbols

possibly decorated at the end by primes and/or digits (representing subscripts). Hyphens are for separating parts of long descriptive identifiers, though capitalization can also be used. Letter case and all characters are significant, so that the following are all different identifiers:

    Price-of-Tea   PriceOfTea   price-of-tea   PRICE-OF-TEA

Different styles can be used conventionally to distinguish different classes of identifiers. In this book the following conventions for capitalization are generally used:

- all small letters (as price-of-tea): composite type tags, local variables, error conditions, functions, loop indexes, pattern identifiers, and implicit function and operation results;

- first letter (or first letter of each word) capital, rest small (as Price-of-tea or Price-Of-Tea): modules, types;

- all capital letters (as PRICE-OF-TEA): record fields, operators, state variables.

Table 3 Symbolic literals

literal	type	values	example	section
Boolean literal	$\mathbb{B}$	truth values	**true**	4.2
numeric literal	$\mathbb{Q}$	integers and decimal fractions	666	4.3
character literal	**char**	graphic characters	'X'	4.4
text literal	**char***	character sequences	"Marilyn"	4.4
quote literal	quote type	a quote value	FORWARDS	4.5
nil literal	nil type	the nil value	**nil**	5.7

2.3 Lexical Structure – Symbols

Table 4 Implicitly declared identifiers

identifier	declaration of Id	section
inv-Id	type definition or state definition	3.2, 3.4
init-Id	state definition	3.4
is-Id	any type definition	3.2
mk-Id	composite type definition	5.5
pre-Id	implicit function or operation definition	7.2, 8.2
post-Id	implicit function or operation definition	7.2, 8.2

Table 5 Keywords and compound delimiters

keywords

abs	all	always	as
be	by	card	cases
char	compose	conc	dcl
def	defined	definitions	div
do	dom	elems	else
elseif	end	error	errs
exit	exports	ext	false
floor	for	from	functions
hd	if	imports	in
inds	init	instantiation	inv
is	len	let	merge
mod	module	nil	not
of	operations	others	parameters
post	pre	rd	rem
return	reverse	rng	-set
skip	st	state	then
tixe	tl	to	token
trap	true	types	undefined
using	values	while	with
wr	yet		

compound delimiters

::   :=   ...   ∃!   --   ""   *mk*-

17

2.4 Comments

2.4.1 Syntax

   comment = '--', {character - newline}, newline;

2.4.2 Meaning

Two ways of mixing VDM-SL and other text are available.

A *comment* is intended as a note at the end of a line, or a short note of a few lines; it is introduced by -- and runs to the end of the line (repeated as necessary).

Longer sections of non-VDM-SL text, whether long comments or sections of text within which sections of VDM-SL text are embedded, are also allowed; they are called *annotations*. How they are distinguished is a matter of lexical presentation; some possibilities are: by a characteristic of the typeface, by a marginal marking, or by delimiters (as with the ISO 646 syntax, see Appendix B).

2.4.3 Examples

See Appendix C for examples of both forms.

3 Overall Structure

3.1 Documents and definitions

3.1.1 Syntax

document = module list | definition block list;

definition block list = definition block, {definition block};

definition block = type definition block | state definition
 | value definition block | function definition block
 | operation definition block;

3.1.2 Meaning

The highest level of construct of the language is a *document*, which is intended to represent a unit in some outer context. Two types of document are available, to allow different styles of writing. In the more structured style, a document is a sequence of 1 or more modules (a *module list*), a *module* being a fairly self-contained unit with an identifier, an interface part defining the external properties of the module, and a set of definitions. This style is described in chapter 10. A freer style is available where a document is just a sequence of definitions (a *definition block list*), grouped into *definition blocks*; this is called the *flat language* and is almost independent of the structuring features. The flat language is described in chapters 3 to 9 inclusive.

In the flat language, a declaration for which the scope is the entire document is said to have *global scope*. This simple picture is modified in the structured language, which has features for controlling the use of names across modules; see chapter 10.

3.2 Types and type definitions

3.2.1 Syntax

   type definition block = **'types'**, type definition, {';', type definition};

   type definition =
      identifier, '=', type expression, [invariant definition]
      | identifier, '::', field list, [invariant definition]
      | identifier, **'is'**, **'not'**, **'yet'**, **'defined'**;

   type expression =
      bracketed type expression | type name | basic type expression
      | quote type expression | composite type expression
      | union type expression | set type expression
      | sequence type expression | map type expression
      | function type expression | optional type expression
      | product type expression | type variable;

   bracketed type expression = '(', type expression, ')';

   type name = name;

   invariant definition = **'inv'**, pattern, '$\underline{\triangle}$', expression;

   type variable = type variable identifier;

   type membership expression = identifier, '(', expression, ')'
      | basic type membership identifier, '(', expression, ')';

3.2.2 Meaning

Types are sets of values. They are used to define the possible values of expressions and to constrain the values that are allowed in particular contexts.

There are a number of *basic types* that are predefined: for example numbers and characters; see chapter 4. There are also various *type constructors* that allow new *compound types* to be defined; see chapter 5.

Every type may be considered to have an additional *undefined value*, which arises for example through use of an operator on an operand for which it is not defined, for example 1/0. Most expressions are *strict* on undefined values; the existence of any operand with an undefined value is enough to make the value of the expression also undefined. Composite and quantified expressions and Boolean expressions are exceptions, to allow

3.2 Overall Structure – Types and type definitions

the effect of undefined values to be confined and not spread out to devastate an entire specification.

The simplest form of *type definition* has the form:

   Id = T

where Id is an identifier and T is a type expression. This is a declaration of Id as denoting T with global scope. It may be followed by an invariant definition, see below. A special form with :: is available for composite types, see section 5.5.

An *invariant definition* in a type definition takes the form:

   inv Pt $\triangleq$ B

where Pt is a pattern (see section 6.2) of the type being defined, and B is a Boolean expression. The invariant is a condition which limits the values of the defined type to those for which B is **true** when evaluated for the bindings from the matching of Pt to that value (see section 6.2). The scope of the pattern identifiers in Pt is the expression B. The expression B must not be loosely specified.

The invariant definition, if present, defines a function on parameters of the type defined by T (without the invariant):

   inv-Id : T $\rightarrow$ $\mathbb{B}$
   inv-Id(Pt) $\triangleq$ B

Types can also be defined *recursively*, by a system of type definitions:

   $Id_1 = T_1$
   $Id_2 = T_2$
   ...
   $Id_n = T_n$

where some or all of the identifiers Id_i occur in the type expressions T_i; the type definitions may also include invariants. These type equations must satisfy a certain continuity criterion to ensure that they define a set of valid non-empty types; see the Standard for details. Most normal usage satisfies the criterion provided that there is a path through the recursion for each type expression T_i which terminates on a defined type.

3.2 Overall Structure – Types and type definitions

Two general forms of type expression T are:

- a type name Nm (in the flat language this is just an identifier); this denotes the previously defined type denoted by Nm;

- a bracketed type expression (T); this denotes the same type as T.

A type can be introduced and named, but not defined, by an *incomplete type definition* of the form:

   Id **is not yet defined**

This indicates that the type definition will be supplied later. It should not be used for a type which is to be left unspecified at the present stage of development, for which **token** is available. There is no constraint on the use of the type identifier Id, though when the type definition is supplied it must of course be consistent with all uses.

Type variables (which have the form of identifiers beginning with the special character @) are used only in *polymorphic function definitions*, see section 7.5; they must not be used anywhere else.

The type of a value E can be tested by a *type membership expression* of the form:

   is-T(E)

where T is a type name and E is an expression of any type. For a basic type, *is*-T is a predefined delimiter, for example *is*-$\mathbb{Z}$(E) tests whether E is an integer. For a named type T, *is*-T is implicitly declared with the type definition; for a composite type T may also be the tag identifier. If T_1 is the union type $T_2 \mid T_3$, then *is*-$T_1(x)$ = *is*-$T_2(x)$ ∨ *is*-$T_3(x)$. There is no type membership expression for a quote type QT; the same result can be achieved by using the equality operator: E = QT.

3.2.3 Examples

It is usually good practice to define all types which are used more than once, and all types involving invariants, and to use their type identifiers thereafter. See Appendix C for many examples.

3.2 Overall Structure – Types and type definitions

Here is an example of a recursive type definition:

    Binary-tree :: *BRANCHES* : [*Binary-tree* × *Binary-tree*]
                VALUE : $\mathbb{R}$

This defines the type of finite binary trees with a numeric value at each node.

An invariant on a recursively defined type need not be expressed recursively; thus to constrain the value at each node of a binary tree to be the mean of the values of all its children, it is enough to have the invariant:

    inv *mk-Binary-tree* (*b*, *v*) $\underline{\triangle}$
        (*b* = **nil**) ∨ **let** *mk-*(*l*, *r*) = *b* **in** *v* = (*l.VALUE* + *r.VALUE*)/2

The corresponding invariant function is:

    inv-Binary-tree : *Binary-tree*' → $\mathbb{B}$
    inv-Binary-tree(*mk-Binary-tree*'(*b*, *v*)) $\underline{\triangle}$
        (*b* = **nil**) ∨ **let** *mk-*(*l*, *r*) = *b* **in** *v* = (*l.VALUE* + *r.VALUE*)/2

where *Binary-tree*' is *Binary-tree* without the invariant:

    Binary-tree' = **compose** *Binary-tree* **of**
                  BRANCHES : [*Binary-tree* × *Binary-tree*]
                  VALUE : $\mathbb{R}$
        end

Type membership expressions can be used for any values: *is-*$\mathbb{Z}$(3) is **true**, *is-*$\mathbb{Z}$(1.5) and *is-*$\mathbb{Z}$("three") are **false**. Type membership expressions are useful in disentangling the types that have been put together in a union type. For example, a type membership expression could be used to find the flavour of a drink *d* (see Appendix C.1):

    if *is-Tea-or-coffee*(*d*)**then** *d.FLAVOUR* **else** CHOCOLATE

3.3 Values and value definitions

3.3.1 Syntax

value definition block = **'values'**, value definition, {';', value definition};

value definition = pattern, [':', type expression], '=', expression
| pattern, [':', type expression], **'is'**, **'not'**, **'yet'**, **'defined'**;

3.3.2 Meaning

A *value definition* has one of the forms:

Pt = E
Pt : T = E

where Pt is a pattern, T is a type expression, and E is an expression. The pattern Pt is matched to the value E, binding any pattern identifiers in Pt to the matching values. The type expression T, if present, restricts the values of E for which the value definition is valid to members of the type T. A value definition declares the pattern identifiers in Pt with global scope.

A value can be named but not defined by an *incomplete value definition* of one of the forms:

Pt **is not yet defined**
Pt : T **is not yet defined**

This means that the matching value will be supplied later. It can be assumed that the value will match Pt; if T is present, then it can also be assumed that the matching value will be a member of T.

3.3.3 Examples

A value acts as a parameterless function returning a constant result. The specification of a set of mathematical functions, for instance, might define the range and accuracy of the results as values.

Values of compound types are also useful. An example is a map value used to define a fixed table of values; see for instance the values *WORTH* (defining the monetary values of coins) and *INGREDIENTS* (defining the ingredients needed for each kind of drink) in the vending machine specification in Appendix C.1.

3.4 The state

3.4.1 Syntax

state definition =
   '**state**', identifier, '**of**', field list,
     [invariant definition],
     [initialization definition],
   '**end**';

invariant definition = '**inv**', pattern, '$\underline{\triangle}$', expression;

initialization definition = '**init**', pattern, '$\underline{\triangle}$', expression;

3.4.2 Meaning

The *state* is the means by which a module retains knowledge of its history of operation calls. The state is defined by a *state definition* of the form:

   state Id **of**
     Fd_1
     Fd_2
     ...
     Fd_n
   end

where Id is an identifier and the Fd_i are *fields* (see section 5.5), and may be thought of as a single instance of a notional record type containing those fields. The fields are called *state variables*. The state definition declares the state identifier Id and the field identifiers Id_i, all with global scope. The state identifier has little use in the flat language, and the field identifiers can be used only within operation bodies. The types of the field identifiers Id_i are the associated field types T_i. The types T_i must all be flat (see section 5.8).

The field list may be empty, though this is not very useful. The fields may be anonymous, in which case they cannot be referred to directly, but only by a pattern match (see section 6.2).

The identifier Id is used to refer to the state in a module document (see chapter 10). In the flat language it is used in the invariant and initialization definitions, but is otherwise just an annotation, and serves to give a name to the specification.

3.4 Overall Structure – The state

An *invariant definition* in a state definition has the form:

    inv Pt ≜ B

where Pt is a pattern (see section 6.2) which has the notional record type of the state, and B is a Boolean expression. The invariant definition defines a condition on the values of the state variables which limits the values of the state variables to those for which B is **true** when evaluated for the bindings of the matching of those values to the components of Pt. B must not be loosely specified.

The invariant definition, if present, defines a function on parameters of the notional state record type T_{Id}:

    $inv\text{-}Id : T_{Id} \rightarrow \mathbb{B}$
    $inv\text{-}Id(Pt) \triangleq B$

An *initialization definition* takes the similar form:

    init Pt ≜ B

where Pt and B are as for an invariant definition. B defines a condition on the values of the state variables before any operation calls.

The initialization definition, if present, defines a function on parameters of the notional state record type T_{Id}:

    $init\text{-}Id : T_{Id} \rightarrow \mathbb{B}$
    $init\text{-}Id(Pt) \triangleq B$

In both an invariant and an initialization definition, Pt must match all combinations of values of the state variables, and B must be defined for all such combinations.

The scope of any pattern identifiers in the invariant or initialization pattern Pt is the following Boolean expression B.

The state invariant acts as a constraint on the types of the state variables. The initial state (so far as it is defined) must satisfy the state invariant, as well as any invariants on the variable types; that is, there must be at least one set of values that satisfies both the initialization condition and the invariant. Similarly each operation must preserve the state invariant: if it is true of the state before the operation then it must be true of at least one possible set of values of the state after the operation.

3.4.3 Examples

A simple example is in section 1.3:

    state *Vending-Machine-1* **of**
        BALANCE : *Money*
        PRICES : *Drink* $\xrightarrow{m}$ *Money*
        inv *mk-Vending-Machine-1(−, c)* $\triangleq$ $\forall$ *d* : *Drink* · *d* $\in$ **dom** *c*
        init *mk-Vending-Machine-1(c, −)* $\triangleq$ *c* = 0
    end

Here *c* denotes *PRICES* in the invariant definition and *BALANCE* in the initialization definition.

It is usually good practice to reduce redundancy as far as possible in the state (though not at the expense of readability). For example, if the simple vending machine example in section 1.3 were to be enhanced to cater for certain drinks being unavailable, the state could be enhanced to:

    state *Vending-Machine-1'* **of**
        BALANCE : *Money*
        PRICES : *Drink* $\xrightarrow{m}$ *Money*
        AVAILABLE : *Drink* $\xrightarrow{m}$ $\mathbb{B}$
        inv *mk-Vending-Machine-1'(−, c, a)* $\triangleq$
            $\forall$ *c* : *Drink* · (*c* $\in$ (**dom** *Prices* $\cap$ **dom** *AVAILABLE*))
        init *mk-Vending-Machine-1'(b, −, a)* $\triangleq$
            (*b* = 0) $\wedge$ (*a* = {*d* $\mapsto$ **true** · *d* : *Drink*})

A shorter formulation would be to use the non-existence of a price to indicate that a drink is unavailable, so that *PRICES* becomes a partial map over *Drink*. This just involves removing the invariant definition:

    state *Vending-Machine-1"* **of**
        BALANCE : *Money*
        PRICES : *Drink* $\xrightarrow{m}$ *Money*
        AVAILABLE : *Drink* $\xrightarrow{m}$ $\mathbb{B}$
        init *mk-Vending-Machine-1"(b, −, a)* $\triangleq$ *b* = 0

3.4 Overall Structure – The state

though the precondition of *GET-DRINK* would need tightening to:

pre (*choice* ∈ **dom** *PRICES*) ∧ (*BALANCE* ≥ *PRICES*(*choice*))

The simpler formulation is less flexible; if an operation is added to replenish stocks and so make drinks available again, the prices will have to be reset.

4 Basic and Quote Types

4.1 General

4.1.1 Syntax

   type expression = ... | basic type expression | quote type expression | ... ;

   basic type expression = '$\mathbb{B}$' | '$\mathbb{N}$' | '$\mathbb{N}_1$' | '$\mathbb{Z}$' | '$\mathbb{Q}$' | '$\mathbb{R}$' | **'char'** | **'token'**;

   quote type expression = quote literal;

4.1.2 Meaning

The *basic types* are the types defined by the language, with distinct values that cannot be analysed into simpler values. There are four fundamental basic types: *Booleans*, *real numbers*, *characters*, and *tokens*, and four basic types which are subsets of the real numbers.

The *Boolean type* is $\mathbb{B}$; it consists of the two *truth values* **true** and **false**. See section 4.2.

The *real number type* is $\mathbb{R}$, the set of real numbers. Certain subsets of $\mathbb{R}$ are also predefined: $\mathbb{Q}$ (*rational numbers*), $\mathbb{Z}$ (*integers*), $\mathbb{N}$ (*natural numbers*, or non-negative integers), and $\mathbb{N}_1$ (*positive integers*); see section 4.3. VDM-SL follows the usual mathematical convention of identifying corresponding members of these types: there is no distinction between integer 2 and real (or rational) 2.0, for instance. So $\mathbb{N}_1$ is a subtype of $\mathbb{N}$, $\mathbb{N}$ is a subtype of $\mathbb{Z}$, $\mathbb{Z}$ is a subtype of $\mathbb{Q}$, and $\mathbb{Q}$ is a subtype of $\mathbb{R}$.

The *character type* is **char**; it consists of the graphic characters of the VDM-SL character set — see section 4.4.

4.1 Basic and Quote Types – General

The *token type* is **token**. This consists of a countably infinite set of distinct values, called *tokens*, having no predefined properties except equality and inequality. Tokens cannot be individually represented.

Each basic type T has a corresponding *basic type membership identifier* '*is-T*' which is used to form a *type membership expression* to test whether any value is of type T. See section 3.2.

A *quote type* is a type containing a single value, both the value and the type being represented by the same quote literal. Like tokens, quote values have no properties other than equality and inequality. Quote types are user-defined, rather than language-defined, and so are not classified as basic types. See section 4.5.

For each basic type, and for quote types in general, this chapter gives the type name, the forms of literals, and operators taking operands of that type. Basic and quote types are summarized in Table 6.

4.1.3 Examples

The token type **token** is used to define a type with the minimum of specified properties, for example identifiers in the definition of a programming language, or when it is intended to provide more properties in a later refinement, as for the type *Drink* in section 1.3.

Table 6 Basic and quote types

type	values	section
$\mathbb{B}$	the logical values **true** and **false**	4.2
$\mathbb{N}$	the natural numbers 0, 1, 2, ...	4.3
$\mathbb{N}_1$	the positive integers 1, 2, 3, ...	4.3
$\mathbb{Z}$	the integers ..., −2, −1, 0 ,1 ,2 ,...	4.3
$\mathbb{Q}$	the rational numbers	4.3
$\mathbb{R}$	the real numbers	4.3
char	the VDM-SL character set	4.4
token	the tokens	4.1
quote type QT	the quote value denoted by the quote literal QT	4.5

4.2 Boolean values

4.2.1 Syntax

    basic type expression = ... | $\mathbb{B}$ | ... ;

    boolean literal = **'true'** | **'false'**;

    logical prefix operator = '¬';

    logical infix operator = '∧' | '∨' | '⇒' | '⇔';

    general infix operator '=' | '≠';

4.2.2 Meaning

The values of the *Boolean type* $\mathbb{B}$ are the two *truth values* of classical logic corresponding to truth and falsity, denoted respectively by the two literals of type $\mathbb{B}$, **true** and **false**. Boolean expressions have special rules which allow them to be evaluated in some cases even when one operand has an undefined value; see below.

There is one unary (prefix) Boolean operator, and four binary (infix) Boolean operators. Boolean operators are also called *logical operators*.

- the *negation* of a Boolean expression B ("not B") is:

    ¬ B

    This is **true** if B is **false** and vice versa. Note that ¬¬B ⇔ B.

- The *disjunction* of two Boolean expressions B_1 and B_2 ("B_1 or B_2") is:

    $B_1 \lor B_2$

    This is **true** if B_1 or B_2 (or both) is **true**, and **false** if both B_1 and B_2 are **false**.

- The *conjunction* of B_1 and B_2 ("B_1 and B_2") is:

    $B_1 \land B_2$

4.2 Basic and Quote Types – Boolean values

This is **true** if both B_1 and B_2 are **true**, and **false** if either B_1 or B_2 is **false** (or both are).

- The *implication* of B_2 by B_1 ("B_1 implies B_2") is:

  $B_1 \Rightarrow B_2$

  This is **true** if B_1 is **false** or B_2 is **true** or both, and is **false** only if B_1 is **true** and B_2 is **false**.

- The *equivalence* of B_1 and B_2 ("B_1 is equivalent to B_2") is:

  $B_1 \Leftrightarrow B_2$

  This is **true** if B_1 and B_2 are both **true** or both **false**, and **false** if B_1 is **true** and B_2 is **false** or vice versa.

- *Equality* and *inequality* are also available, as for all flat types:

  $B_1 = B_2 \qquad B_1 \neq B_2$

  $B_1 = B_2$ is **true** if B_1 and B_2 have the same value and **false** otherwise; it is the same as $B_1 \Leftrightarrow B_2$. $B_1 \neq B_2$ is **true** if $B_1 = B_2$ is **false**, and vice versa.

Boolean operators are summarized in Table 7. Truth tables for the operators are given in Table 8.

Other operators giving Boolean values are:

- arithmetic comparisons, see section 4.3;
- set membership and inclusion, see section 5.2;
- equality and inequality, see section 6.3;
- quantified expressions, see section 6.6;
- type membership expressions, see section 3.2.

The usual necessity for all operands of an expression to have defined values is modified for Boolean expressions, to allow for cases where it is not necessary to evaluate all operands to find the value of the expression.

4.2 Basic and Quote Types – Boolean values

The rules are shown in Table 8, where U stands for an operand which has an undefined value.

4.2.3 Examples

The other logical operations can be defined in terms of $\neg$ and any one other operator, for example:

$$B_1 \wedge B_2 = \neg (\neg B_1 \vee \neg B_2)$$
$$B_1 \Rightarrow B_2 = \neg B_1 \vee B_2$$
$$(B_1 \Leftrightarrow B_2) = \neg (\neg B_1 \vee \neg B_2) \vee \neg (B_1 \vee B_2)$$

Equivalence and equality are semantically identical for Boolean values. Equivalence is generally used in Boolean expressions, except where the context makes equality more natural. For instance one term of a postcondition which happened to be Boolean might be better expressed using equality:

post $(n = \overleftarrow{n} + 1) \wedge (b = \neg \overleftarrow{b}) \wedge (s = \overleftarrow{s} \cup \{n\})$

The special rules for undefined values in Boolean expressions allow for example the use of the expression:

$(x = 0) \vee (1/x = 1)$

for all values of x in $\mathbb{R}$, despite the fact that $1/x = 1$ cannot be evaluated if $x = 0$ (the expression is **true** if x is 0 or 1 and **false** otherwise).

Another example is the application of a map to a value that might lie outside its domain:

if $(v \in \mathbf{dom}\ m) \wedge (m(v) > 10)$ **then** A **else** B

The difficulty here is that if $v \notin \mathbf{dom}\ m$ then $m(v)$ is undefined, and with the classical definition of $\wedge$ this makes the whole expression undefined. In some dialects it is necessary to get round this problem by writing:

if $v \in \mathbf{dom}\ m$ **then** (**if** $m(v) > 10$ **then** A **else** B) **else** B

33

4.2 Basic and Quote Types – Boolean values

This is not necessary in standard VDM-SL as the value of the Boolean expression is well defined.

Table 7 Logical operators

operator	signature & meaning
$\neg\, B_2$	$\mathbb{B} \rightarrow \mathbb{B}$; negation of B_2
$B_1 \vee B_2$	$\mathbb{B} \times \mathbb{B} \rightarrow \mathbb{B}$; disjunction of B_1 and B_2
$B_1 \wedge B_2$	$\mathbb{B} \times \mathbb{B} \rightarrow \mathbb{B}$; conjunction of B_1 and B_2
$B_1 \Rightarrow B_2$	$\mathbb{B} \times \mathbb{B} \rightarrow \mathbb{B}$; implication of B_2 by B_1
$B_1 \Leftrightarrow B_2$	$\mathbb{B} \times \mathbb{B} \rightarrow \mathbb{B}$; equivalence of B_1 and B_2
$B_1 = B_2$	$\mathbb{B} \times \mathbb{B} \rightarrow \mathbb{B}$; equality of B_1 and B_2
$B_1 \neq B_2$	$\mathbb{B} \times \mathbb{B} \rightarrow \mathbb{B}$; inequality of B_1 and B_2

Table 8 Truth tables for the logical operators (T = **true**, F = **false**, U = undefined)

B_1	B_2	$\neg B_1$	$B_1 \vee B_2$	$B_1 \wedge B_2$	$B_1 \Rightarrow B_2$	$B_1 \Leftrightarrow B_2$	$B_1 = B_2$	$B_1 \neq B_2$
T	T	F	T	T	T	T	T	F
T	F	F	T	F	F	F	F	T
T	U	F	T	U	U	U	U	U
F	T	T	T	F	T	F	F	T
F	F	T	F	F	T	T	T	F
F	U	T	U	F	T	U	U	U
U	T	U	T	U	T	U	U	U
U	F	U	U	F	U	U	U	U
U	U	U	U	U	U	U	U	U

4.3 Numeric values

4.3.1 Syntax

basic type expression = ... | N | N$_1$ | Z | Q | R | ... ;

numeric literal = numeral, ['.', digit, {digit}], [exponent];

numeral = digit, {digit};

exponent = '×10↑', ['+' | '−'], numeral;

arithmetic prefix operator = '+' | '−' | **'abs'** | **'floor'**;

arithmetic infix operator = '+' | '−' | '×' | '/' | '↑' | **'rem'** | **'mod'**
 | **'div'** | '<' | '≤' | '>' | '≥';

general infix operator = '=' | '≠';

4.3.2 Meaning

The values of the *real number type* R are the *real numbers* (positive, negative, and zero) of mathematics. The other numeric types are successively more restricted subsets of R, as follows.

Q : *rational numbers* $\frac{m}{n}$ where *m* and *n* are integers, $n \neq 0$

Z : *integers* (positive, negative, and zero)

N : *natural numbers* (non-negative integers)

N$_1$: *positive integers* (1, 2, 3, ...)

At this level of abstraction, no complications of accuracy and range arise in the language definition: all operators are mathematically exact and all types are infinite. Any accuracy or range constraints must be expressed within the language.

The available literals are for a subset of Q: the *decimal fractions*, or rational values $\frac{m}{10^n}$ for $n \geq 0$, *m* any integer, represented in the conventional decimal notation.

The *numeric literal*

$d_0 \, d_1 \, ... \, d_n$

4.3 Basic and Quote Types – Numeric values

represents the integer $d_0 \cdot 10^n + d_1 \cdot 10^{n-1} + \ldots + d_n$, where each digit d_i stands for the corresponding integer.

The *numeric literal*

$$d_0 d_1 \ldots d_n \cdot e_1 e_2 \ldots e_m$$

represents the rational number $d_0 \cdot 10^n + d_1 \cdot 10^{n-1} + \ldots + d_n + e_1 \cdot 10^{-1} + e_2 \cdot 10^{-2} + \ldots + e_m \cdot 10^{-m}$.

The effect of an *exponent* ×10↑Z is to multiply the value represented by 10^Z.

The usual arithmetic operations are provided.

- The unary (prefix) operators are *unary plus* (or *identity*) and *unary minus* (or *negation*):

    +X   -X

    The former has no effect (the value is the same as that of X: +X = X always); it is provided for completeness and symmetry with unary minus. The latter negates the value of its operand: if $X_1 = -1.5$ and $X_2 = 3$ then $-X_1 = 1.5$ and $-X_2 = -3$. Note that $-0 = 0$, and $-(-X) = X$ always.

- The *absolute value* operator is:

    abs X

    This returns the absolute value of the operand X: the positive or zero value with the same magnitude as X. If $X_1 = -1.5$ and $X_2 = 3$, then **abs** $X_1 = 1.5$ and **abs** $X_2 = 3$.

- The *floor* or *integer part* operator is:

    floor X

    It returns the greatest (most positive) integer value not greater than X. If $X_1 = -1.5$ and $X_2 = 3$, **floor** $X_1 = -2$ and **floor** $X_2 = 3$.

4.3 Basic and Quote Types – Numeric values

- The binary (infix) operators include *addition* (or *plus*), *subtraction* (or *minus*), *multiplication* (or *times*), *division*, and *exponentiation* (or *to the power of*):

$$X_1 + X_2 \qquad X_1 - X_2 \qquad X_1 \times X_2 \qquad X_1 / X_2 \qquad X_1 \uparrow X_2$$

with the usual arithmetic meanings. If $X_1 = -1.5$ and $X_2 = 3$, then $X_1 + X_2 = 1.5$, $X_1 - X_2 = -4.5$, $X_1 \times X_2 = -4.5$, $X_1 / X_2 = -0.5$, and $X_1 \uparrow X_2 = -3.375$. X_1 / X_2 is defined only if $X_2 \neq 0$. $X_1 \uparrow X_2$ is defined only in the cases:

- $X_1 > 0$, all values of X_2: if $X_1 > 0$ then $X_1 \uparrow X_2 > 0$ always;

- $X_1 = 0$, $X_2 > 0$: if $X_2 > 0$ then $0 \uparrow X_2 = 0$;

- $X_1 < 0$, X_2 integral (a member of $\mathbb{Z}$).

In particular $X_1 \uparrow 0 = 1$ if $X_1 \neq 0$, but $0 \uparrow 0$ is undefined. If $X_1 > 0$ then $(-X_1) \uparrow Z_2 = X_1 \uparrow Z_2$ if Z_2 is even, $-(X_1 \uparrow Z_2)$ if Z_2 is odd.

- There are three binary operators concerning division that are defined for integer operands only; *integer division*, *remainder*, and *modulus*:

$$Z_1 \text{ div } Z_2 \qquad Z_1 \text{ rem } Z_2 \qquad Z_1 \text{ mod } Z_2$$

Z_1 **div** Z_2 and Z_1 **rem** Z_2 are the integer quotient and remainder for integer division; Z_1 **mod** Z_2 is the so-called modulus. They are all undefined if $Z_2 = 0$.

The integer quotient Z_1 **div** Z_2 is positive if Z_1 and Z_2 have the same sign and negative otherwise. It is the next integer below the real quotient Z_1/Z_2 in absolute value:

$$\textbf{abs } (Z_1 \textbf{ div } Z_2) = \textbf{abs floor } (Z_1/Z_2)$$

Z_1 **rem** Z_2 is the true remainder for integer division, while Z_1 **mod** Z_2 is a generalization of the concept of residue from number theory. Z_1 **rem** Z_2 and Z_1 **mod** Z_2 differ only if Z_1 and Z_2 have different signs: Z_1 **rem** Z_2 takes the sign of Z_1 and Z_1 **mod** Z_2 takes

4.3 Basic and Quote Types – Numeric values

the sign of Z_2. They have integer values always, and are connected by the following relations, where *sign (Z)* denotes the sign of Z. See Table 10 for examples of their values.

- $Z_1 = Z_2 \times (Z_1 \text{ div } Z_2) + Z_1 \text{ rem } Z_2$
- $sign(Z_1 \text{ rem } Z_2) = sign(Z_1)$
- $abs(Z_1 \text{ rem } Z_2) < abs\, Z_2$

- $Z_1 = Z_2 \times floor(Z_1/Z_2) + (Z_1 \text{ mod } Z_2)$
- $sign(Z_1 \text{ mod } Z_2) = sign(Z_2)$
- $abs(Z_1 \text{ mod } Z_2) < abs\, Z_2$

- Finally there are six *comparison operators* giving Boolean results: *equality* and *inequality*:

$X_1 = X_2 \qquad X_1 \neq X_2$

which are **true** and **false** respectively if X_1 and X_2 have the same value, and **false** and **true** respectively otherwise; and the *ordering operators*: less than, less than or equal to, greater than, and greater than or equal to:

$X_1 < X_2 \qquad X_1 \leq X_2 \qquad X_1 > X_2 \qquad X_1 \geq X_2$

each of which is **true** if X_1 bears the specified relation to X_2 and **false** otherwise. If $X_1 = -1.5$ and $X_2 = 3$, then $X_1 \neq X_2$, $X_1 < X_2$, and $X_1 \leq X_2$ are **true**; $X_1 = X_2$, $X_1 > X_2$, and $X_1 \geq X_2$ are **false**.

The numeric operators (also called *arithmetic operators*) are summarized in Table 9. They are all strict on undefined values, so if the operand of a unary operator, or either operand of a binary operator, is undefined, so is the result.

4.3.3 Examples

There is no distinction between the values represented by integer and rational literals: the integer literal 42 and the rational literal $0.42 \times 10\uparrow 2$ represent the same value, which is both an integer and a rational number.

Leading and trailing zeros are allowed and have no significance: 00042 and $4200.00 \times 10\uparrow -02$ both denote 42.

4.3 Basic and Quote Types – Numeric values

Only rational numbers with values $m \times 10^n$ for integral m and n can be represented as literals. Other rational numbers, for example $\frac{1}{3}$, can be represented as expressions: 1/3. Irrational numbers cannot be represented literally, but can still be handled: the value of *sqrt* (2) is √2, where:

sqrt $(x : \mathbb{R})r : \mathbb{R}$
pre $x \geq 0$
post $(r \geq 0) \land (r \uparrow 2 = x)$

A more realistic specification of a square root function gives an example of control of precision: *sqrt-2* returns an approximation to the square root of its argument with relative accuracy ε.

sqrt-2$(x : \mathbb{R})r : \mathbb{R}$
pre $x \geq 0$
post $(r \geq 0) \land$ **let** $y = sqrt\ (x)$ **in abs** $((r - y)/y) \leq \varepsilon$

The only rounding operator provided is **floor**, which converts a real number to the largest integer not greater than it. Its partner "ceiling", and more general rounding functions, are easily defined in terms of **floor**:

ceiling $: \mathbb{R} \to \mathbb{Z}$
ceiling$(x) \triangleq -$ **floor** $(-x)$

trunc $: \mathbb{R} \times \mathbb{N}_1 \to \mathbb{Q}$
trunc$(x, n) \triangleq$ **if** $x \geq 0$ **then floor**$(x \times 10\uparrow n)/10\uparrow n$
                         else *ceiling*$(x \times 10\uparrow n)/10\uparrow n$
-- truncate x towards 0 to n decimal places

Since all numeric values are members of $\mathbb{R}$, there is no question of overloading: the same operator operates on real numbers, rational numbers, etc. The result is always of type $\mathbb{R}$; whether it is of one of the other numeric types depends on its value. Thus 3·6/1·8 and 0·2 × 10 both have the value 2, of type $\mathbb{N}_1$. This is true also of functions and operations; for example the function *sum* giving the sum of a set of positive integers:

4.3 Basic and Quote Types – Numeric values

$sum(s : \mathbb{N}_1\text{-}\mathbf{set}) \triangleq \mathbf{if}\ s = \{\ \}\ \mathbf{then}\ 0$
  $\mathbf{else\ let}\ n \in s\ \mathbf{in}\ n + sum(s - \{n\})$

(see Appendix C.1) could equally well be defined for all real numbers:

$sum(s : \mathbb{R}\text{-}\mathbf{set}) \triangleq \mathbf{if}\ s = \{\ \}\ \mathbf{then}\ 0$
  $\mathbf{else\ let}\ x \in s\ \mathbf{in}\ x + sum(s - \{x\})$

The application of *sum* to integers would not be affected.

4.3 Basic and Quote Types – Numeric values

Table 9 Numeric operations

operator	signature & value
+ X	$\mathbb{R} \to \mathbb{R}$; X
- X	$\mathbb{R} \to \mathbb{R}$; negation of X, minus X: 0 - X
abs X	$\mathbb{R} \to \mathbb{R}$; absolute value of X: **if** X<0 **then** -X **else** X
floor X	$\mathbb{R} \to \mathbb{Z}$; greatest integer not greater than X
$X_1 + X_2$	$\mathbb{R} \times \mathbb{R} \to \mathbb{R}$; sum of X_1 added to X_2, X_1 plus X_2
$X_1 - X_2$	$\mathbb{R} \times \mathbb{R} \to \mathbb{R}$; difference of X_2 subtracted from X_1, X_1 minus X_2
$X_1 \times X_2$	$\mathbb{R} \times \mathbb{R} \to \mathbb{R}$; product of X_1 and X_2, X_1 times X_2
X_1 / X_2	$\mathbb{R} \times \mathbb{R} \to \mathbb{R}$; quotient of X_1 divided by X_2, X_1 over X_2; $X_2 \neq 0$
Z_1 **mod** Z_2	$\mathbb{Z} \times \mathbb{Z} \to \mathbb{Z}$; modulus: see above; $Z_2 \neq 0$
Z_1 **rem** Z_2	$\mathbb{Z} \times \mathbb{Z} \to \mathbb{Z}$; remainder: see above; $Z_2 \neq 0$
Z_1 **div** Z_2	$\mathbb{Z} \times \mathbb{Z} \to \mathbb{Z}$; integer division: see above; $Z_2 \neq 0$
$X_1 \uparrow X_2$	$\mathbb{R} \times \mathbb{R} \to \mathbb{R}$; X_1 raised to X_2th power; for constraints see above
$X_1 < X_2$	$\mathbb{R} \times \mathbb{R} \to \mathbb{B}$; X_1 is less than X_2
$X_1 > X_2$	$\mathbb{R} \times \mathbb{R} \to \mathbb{B}$; X_1 is greater than X_2
$X_1 \leq X_2$	$\mathbb{R} \times \mathbb{R} \to \mathbb{B}$; X_1 is not greater than X_2
$X_1 \geq X_2$	$\mathbb{R} \times \mathbb{R} \to \mathbb{B}$; X_1 is not less than X_2
$X_1 = X_2$	$\mathbb{R} \times \mathbb{R} \to \mathbb{B}$; X_1 is equal to X_2
$X_1 \neq X_2$	$\mathbb{R} \times \mathbb{R} \to \mathbb{B}$; X_1 is not equal to X_2

Table 10 Values of **rem**, **div**, and **mod**

Z_1	Z_2	Z_1 **rem** Z_2	Z_1 **div** Z_2	Z_1 **mod** Z_2	floor(Z_1/Z_2)
+14	+3	+2	+4	+2	+4
+14	-3	+2	-4	-1	-5
-14	+3	-2	-4	+1	-5
-14	-3	-2	+4	-2	+4

4.4 Characters

4.4.1 Syntax

    basic type expression = ... | **'char'** | ... ;

    character literal = " ' ", character - separator, " ' ";

    text literal = ' " ', {' "" ' | character - (' " ' | separator)}, ' " ';

    general infix operator = '=' | '≠';

4.4.2 Meaning

Values of the *character type* **char**, called *characters*, are the elements of the VDM-SL character set; see section 2.2. Characters have no further structure.

The character literal 'χ', where χ is a graphic character, denotes that character; thus '@' denotes the character @.

The only operators on characters are equality and inequality: $X_1 = X_2$ is **true** if X_1 and X_2 are the same character and **false** otherwise; and vice versa for $X_1 \neq X_2$. In particular, characters are not ordered.

Sequences of characters are called *text strings*; they are values of the sequence type **char*** (or **char**$^+$ for nonempty text strings; see section 5.4). There is a special literal notation for text strings: the *text literal* "$\chi_1\chi_2...\chi_n$" ($n \geq 0$) denotes the same sequence of characters $\chi_1\chi_2...\chi_n$ as ['χ_1', 'χ_2', ..., 'χ_n'], except that within a text literal the character " is denoted by repeating it to form the compound delimiter: "" .

4.4.3 Examples

Examples of text literals:

    "Brigitte"   denotes ['B', 'r', 'i', 'g', 'i', 't', 't', 'e']

    " "   denotes [ ] (the empty sequence)

    "A""string"""   denotes ['A', ' " ', 's', 't', 'r', 'i', 'n', 'g', ' " ']

A function for converting a non-negative integer into a decimal numeral, for example to display the balance on the vending machine of Appendix C.1:

display : $\mathbb{N}$ → **char**$^+$

display(*n*) ≜
  let *ch* = λ *d* ∈ {0, ..., 9} · "0123456789"(*d*) **in**
    if *n* < 10 **then** [*ch*(*n*)]
    else *display* (*n* **div** 10) ⁀ [*ch*(*n* **rem** 10)]

4.5 Quote types

4.5.1 Syntax

   quote type expression = quote literal;

   general infix operator = '=' | '≠';

   quote literal = distinguished letter, {'-' | distinguished letter};

4.5.2 Meaning

The sole value of a *quote type* denoted by a *quote literal* is an elementary *quote value* also denoted by the same quote literal. Quote values have no predefined operations except equality and inequality; two quote literals denote the same value if and only if they are the same.

Quote literals are sequences of DISTINGUISHED LETTERS (which are used for no other purpose) and hyphens, starting with a distinguished letter; for distinguished letters see section 2.2.

4.5.3 Examples

Quote types are almost always used as parts of type unions (see section 5.7). Unions of quote types are useful for small sets of distinct values with no particular ordering, for example:

   Device = TERMINAL | PRINTER | DATA-LINK

Here each of the quote literals TERMINAL, PRINTER, and DATA-LINK stands for the type containing just that one value, so that the type *Device* consists of the three quote values.

A quote literal always denotes the same value (unlike for example enumeration literals in Ada), so that unions of quote types can overlap. Thus in:

   Light = RED | AMBER | GREEN | RED-AND-AMBER
   Colour = RED | GREEN | BLUE

the values RED and GREEN belong to both types.

5 Compound Types

5.1 General

5.1.1 Syntax

type expression = ... | set type expression | map type expression
  | sequence type expression | composite type expression
  | product type expression | union type expression
  | optional type expression | function type expression | ... ;

5.1.2 Meaning

Compound types are types constructed from other types (and at the bottom level from basic types). The *type constructors* are summarized in Table 11.

This chapter describes each compound type, the value constructors used to create values of the type, and operators applicable to it.

The type constructors have their own system of *precedence* and *association*, similar to that for expressions (see section 6.3) but independent of it. This is shown in Table 11; the operation type constructor $\xrightarrow{o}$ is also included (see chapter 8). Precedence goes from 1 (weak) to 4 (strong), and association is L (left), R (right), or X (none). See section 6.3 for further explanation.

Function types and types constructed from them are subject to certain special restrictions: see section 5.8. In particular, a set type T-**set** cannot be constructed if the type T is not *flat*, that is, if it is a function type or a compound type involving a function type. Similarly a map type $T_1 \xrightarrow{m} T_2$ or $T_1 \xleftrightarrow{m} T_2$ cannot be constructed if the domain type T_1 is not flat. The elements of flat types are called *flat values*.

5.1.3 Examples

As an example of the precedence and association rules, the type expression:

$T1 \times T2\text{-}\mathbf{set} \times T3^* \rightarrow T1 \mid T2 \rightarrow T3$

45

5.1 Compound Types – General

means the same as:

$$(T1 \times (T2\text{-}\mathbf{set}) \times (T3^*)) \rightarrow ((T1 \mid T2) \rightarrow T3)$$

This is a nonflat type, as it involves function types. Basic and quote types, and types constructed from them not using function types, are flat; for example the following type is flat:

$$(\mathbb{N} \times \mathbf{token\text{-}set} \times \mathbf{char}^*) \xrightarrow{m} (\text{RED} \mid \text{GREEN}) \xleftrightarrow{m} \mathbb{B}$$

Note the parentheses needed to give the same structure as the previous type expression because of the high precedence of $\xrightarrow{m}$ and $\xleftrightarrow{m}$. In particular, as $\xrightarrow{m}$ and $\xleftrightarrow{m}$ have the same precedence as × but different associations, type expressions such as $T1 \times T2 \xrightarrow{m} T3$ are ambiguous and so illegal, and must be written as $(T1 \times T2) \xrightarrow{m} T3$ or $T1 \times (T2 \xrightarrow{m} T3)$.

5.1 Compound Types – General

Table 11 Compound type expressions

type expression	prec.	assoc.	Type and values
T-**set**	4	X	set type: finite sets of elements of T (including the empty set); T must be flat
$T_1 \xrightarrow{m} T_2$	3	R	map type: all finite maps from T_1 to T_2; T_1 must be flat
$T_1 \xleftrightarrow{m} T_2$	3	R	map type: finite injective maps from T_1 to T_2; T_1 must be flat
T^*	4	X	sequence type: finite sequences of elements of T (including the empty sequence)
T^+	4	X	sequence type: finite sequences of elements of T (excluding the empty sequence)
compose Id **of** $\quad$ $Id_1: T_1$ $\quad$ $Id_2: T_2$ $\quad$ ... $\quad$ $Id_n: T_n$ **end**	-	X	composite type: composite values, containing one element of each of the types $T_1, T_2, ..., T_n$ in order. The Id_i may be omitted (all or nothing)
$T_1 \times T_2 \times ...$	3	X	product type (Cartesian product): ordered tuples $mk\text{-}(t_1,t_2,...)$ with $t_i \in T_i$
$T_1 \mid T_2$	2	L	union type: all the values of T_1 and of T_2
[T]	-	X	optional type: the values of T and **nil**
$T_1 \to T_2$	1	R	function type: functions from values of type T_1 to values of type T_2
$(\,) \to T_2$	1	R	function type: parameterless functions to values of type T_2
$(\,)\mid T_1 \xrightarrow{o} (\,)\mid T_2$	1	R	operation type: see chapter 8

5.2 Sets

5.2.1 Syntax

    set type expression = type expression, '-**set**';

    set expression = set enumeration | set comprehension
        | set range expression;

    set enumeration = '{', [expression list], '}';

    set comprehension = '{', expression, '|', bind list,
        ['·', expression], '}';

    set range expression = '{', expression, ',', '...', ',', expression, '}';

    set prefix operator = '**card**' | '$\mathcal{F}$' | '∪' | '∩';

    set infix operator = '∪' | '∩' | '−' | '⊆' | '⊂' | '∈' | '∉';

    general infix operator = '=' | '≠';

5.2.2 Meaning

A *set* is a collection of distinct values treated as a whole. All sets in VDM-SL are finite: each set contains only a finite number of elements.

If T is a flat type, the *set type*:

    T-**set**

has values which are the finite sets of values of the type T. T can be any flat type (see section 5.8), including a set type; thus $\mathbb{N}_1$-**set-set** (sets of sets of positive integers) and **char**$^+$-**set** (sets of non-empty character strings) are both valid types.

A set value can be constructed either directly by means of a set enumeration or indirectly by means of a set comprehension.

A *set enumeration* has the form:

    {E_1, E_2, ..., E_n}

where E_1, E_2, ... E_n, are expressions all with flat values, and denotes the set containing the values of the expressions E_i. The values of the E_i may well not all be different, in which case the set contains fewer than *n* elements; thus {1, 4, 6, 4, 1} is the same set as {6, 4, 1}.

5.2 Compound Types – Sets

If $n = 0$, the set enumeration is:

{ }

which denotes the *empty set* containing no elements. The empty set is a value of every set type (unless excluded by an invariant). For example, as a value of type *Ingredient*-**set** it represents the ingredients of the familiar null drink (an empty cup).

A *set comprehension* has one of the forms:

$\{E \mid Bd_1, Bd_2, ..., Bd_n \cdot B\}$
$\{E \mid Bd_1, Bd_2, ..., Bd_n\}$

where E is an expression, each Bd_i is either a set bind $Pt_i \in S$ or a type bind $Pt_i : T$ (see section 6.2), and B is a Boolean expression. It denotes the set containing the values of E, evaluated for the bindings from each combination of matching values from $Bd_1, Bd_2, ..., Bd_n$ for which the value of B is **true** (not **false** nor **undefined**). If B is not supplied, as in the second form, the default is **true**, and the set contains the values of E for all combinations of matching values. The scope of any pattern identifiers in the binds Bd_i is the two expressions E and B; if the same pattern identifier occurs more than once, only sets of bindings in which it is bound to the same value are considered. A more compact form of bind list is available when a set or type is repeated; see section 6.2.

For the value of a set comprehension to be defined, E must have a flat value for every combination of matchings of the binds; and there must be only a finite number of different values of E arising from such matchings. The latter condition is always satisfied if all the binds Bd_i are set binds, but may need to be proved if the set comprehension includes one or more type binds.

A special form of set comprehension is the *set range expression*:

$\{X_1, ..., X_2\}$

where X_1 and X_2 are numeric expressions (usually integers); this denotes the set of integers in the closed interval from X_1 to X_2:

$\{n \mid n \in \mathbb{Z} \cdot X_1 \leq n \land n \leq X_2\}$

5.2 Compound Types – Sets

So $\{0,...,5\} = \{i \mid i : \mathbb{N} \cdot i < 6\}$, or $\{0,1,2,3,4,5\}$. The commas and ellipsis here are VDM-SL symbols, not part of the notation. If $X_1 > X_2$ then the set range comprehension denotes the empty set $\{\ \}$.

Operators on sets are as follows; they are summarized in Table 12.

- *Set union*, *set difference*, and *set intersection*, respectively:

$$S_1 \cup S_2 \qquad S_1 - S_2 \qquad S_1 \cap S_2$$

    These operate on two sets S_1 and S_2 to produce another set. $S_1 \cup S_2$ contains the elements in S_1 or in S_2 or in both. $S_1 - S_2$ contains the elements in S_1 but not in S_2. $S_1 \cap S_2$ contains the elements common to S_1 and S_2.

    $\cup$ and $\cap$ are commutative and associative, and distribute over each other:

$$S_1 \cup S_2 = S_2 \cup S_1 \qquad S_1 \cap S_2 = S_2 \cap S_1$$
$$S_1 \cup (S_2 \cup S_3) = (S_1 \cup S_2) \cup S_3$$
$$S_1 \cap (S_2 \cap S_3) = (S_1 \cap S_2) \cap S_3$$
$$S_1 \cup (S_2 \cap S_3) = (S_1 \cup S_2) \cap (S_1 \cup S_3)$$
$$S_1 \cap (S_2 \cup S_3) = (S_1 \cap S_2) \cup (S_1 \cap S_3)$$

    Set difference $-$ is neither commutative nor associative, and does not distribute over $\cup$ or $\cap$; but the following hold:

$$S_1 - (S_2 \cup S_3) = (S_1 - S_2) \cap (S_1 - S_3)$$
$$S_1 - (S_2 \cap S_3) = (S_1 - S_2) \cup (S_1 - S_3)$$

- The *distributed union* and the *distributed intersection* operators:

$$\bigcup S \qquad \bigcap S$$

    take a set S of sets and yield the union and intersection respectively of all its set elements.

- Relations between sets are *equality*, *inequality*, *inclusion* and *proper inclusion*, respectively:

5.2 Compound Types – Sets

$$S_1 = S_2 \qquad S_1 \neq S_2 \qquad S_1 \subseteq S_2 \qquad S_1 \subset S_2$$

$S_1 = S_2$ is **true** if S_1 and S_2 have the same members, and **false** otherwise. So $\{0,...,4\} = \{i \bmod 5 \mid i : \mathbb{Z}\}$ is **true**.

$S_1 \neq S_2$ is **true** if $S_1 = S_2$ is **false** and vice versa.

$S_1 \subseteq S_2$ is **true** if every element of S_1 is an element of S_2 (this includes the possibility that $S_1 = S_2$), and **false** otherwise.

$S_1 \subset S_2$ is **true** if $S_1 \subseteq S_2$ and $S_1 \neq S_2$, so that S_2 has at least one element not in S_1, and **false** otherwise.

For all sets S_1 and S_2, the following hold: $S_1 \subseteq S_1 \cup S_2$, $S_1 - S_2 \subseteq S_1$, $S_1 \cap S_2 \subseteq S_1$. With proper inclusion, the relations are only conditionally true: $(S_1 \subset S_1 \cup S_2) \Leftrightarrow (S_2 - S_1 \neq \{\})$, $(S_1 - S_2 \subset S_1) \Leftrightarrow (S_1 \cap S_2 \neq \{\})$, $(S_1 \cap S_2 \subset S_1) \Leftrightarrow (S_1 - S_2 \neq \{\})$.

- Relations between a value E and a set S are *membership* and *nonmembership*, respectively:

  $$E \in S \qquad E \notin S$$

  $E \in S$ is **true** if the value of E is an element of S, and **false** otherwise. $E \notin S$ is **true** if the value of E is not an element of S, and **false** otherwise; it is the same as $\neg (E \in S)$. So:

  $$(E \in S) \Leftrightarrow (S \cup \{E\} = S) \qquad (E \notin S) \Leftrightarrow (S - \{E\} = S)$$

- The *cardinality* of a set S:

  card S

  is the number of elements of S: **card** $\{\} = 0$, **card** $\{1,2,3\} = 3$, **card** $(S_1 \cup S_2) =$ **card** $S_1 +$ **card** $S_2 -$ **card** $(S_1 \cap S_2)$.

- The *finite subset operator*, which takes a set as operand:

  $\mathcal{F} S$

5.2 Compound Types – Sets

is the inverse of distributed union $\bigcup$, in a sense. It produces the set of all the subsets of its operand: $\mathcal{F}S = \{S' \mid S' : \text{T-set} \cdot S' \subseteq S\}$, where S is of type T-**set**; so $S \subseteq \mathcal{F} \bigcup S$ and $\bigcup \mathcal{F} S = S$. The set of all subsets of a set S is called the *powerset* of S; as in VDM-SL sets are always finite, so are their powersets.

5.2.3 Examples

Sets are the most fundamental compound types, and occur in almost every specification, except perhaps at a low level of abstraction. For instance, in the vending machine specification in Appendix C.1, the map INGREDIENTS maps drinks to sets of ingredients. Sets occur implicitly also as domains and ranges of maps (section 5.3), and as element sets and index sets of sequences (section 5.4). At lower levels of abstraction, sets are often replaced by more concrete data types such as sequences, which are more easily supported by many programming languages.

Set enumerations are suitable for simple cases with few elements:

$\{1,2,3\}$ $\{x + 3, y - 2\}$ $\{\text{TEA, COFFEE, CHOCOLATE}\}$

Set comprehensions are suitable for more complicated cases where it is inconvenient or impossible to enumerate:

$\{n \mid n : \mathbb{N}_1 \cdot (n \bmod 2 = 0) \wedge (n < 100)\}$

is the set of even integers between 2 and 98 inclusive, and:

$\{tri \mid a \frown tri \frown c \in lex \cdot \mathbf{len}\, tri = 3\}$

is the set of all trigrams (3-letter sequences) in the words in a lexicon *lex* (of type $\text{char}^+\text{-set}$). There is often a possible trade-off between the complexity of the expressions E and B of a set comprehension; the above set could also have been written:

$\{[x,y,z] \mid a \frown [x,y,z] \frown c \in lex\}$

Examples of sets and set operators are provided by the vending machine specification in Appendix C.1. Thus the set of sweetened drinks available from the vending machine is:

$\{d \mid d : Drink \cdot \text{SUGAR} \in \text{INGREDIENTS}(d)\}$

5.2 Compound Types – Sets

where *INGREDIENTS(d)* is the set of ingredients of drink *d*.

If *swt* = {TEA, MILK, SUGAR, WATER} of type *Ingredient*-**set** is the set of ingredients for sweet white tea, and *swc* for sweet white coffee, then *swt* ∪ *swc* = {TEA, COFFEE, MILK, SUGAR, WATER}, *swt* − *swc* = {TEA}, and *swt* ∩ *swc* = {MILK, SUGAR, WATER}. Note that (*swt* − *swc*) ∪ (*swt* ∩ *swc*) = *swt*, (*swt* − *swc*) ∩ (*swt* ∩ *swc*) = { }; this is generally true.

If in the vending machine *make-up* is {*INGREDIENTS(d)* | *d* : *Drink*}, then the distributed union ∪*make-up* is the set of all ingredients used in any drink, and the distributed intersection *Ingredients* = ∩*make-up* is the set of ingredients used in all drinks, which is just {WATER}. Finally ℱ*Ingredients* is the set of all possible combinations of ingredients, from the empty set { } of no ingredients, to the set *Ingredients* itself: a concoction of tea, coffee, chocolate, milk, sugar, and water.

5.2 Compound Types – Sets

Table 12 Set operators and expressions

operation	signature & value
$\{E_1, E_2, ..., E_n\}$	$T \times ... \times T \rightarrow$ **T-set**; set enumeration: the set containing $E_1, E_2, ..., E_n$
$\{\ \}$	$(\ ) \rightarrow$ **T-set**; the empty set
$\{E \mid Bd_1, ..., Bd_n \cdot B\}$	$T \times \mathbb{B} \rightarrow$ **T-set**; set comprehension: the set of values of E in the context of Bd_i that satisfy B
$\{X_1, ..., X_2\}$	$\mathbb{R} \times \mathbb{R} \rightarrow$ **Z-set**; integer set range from X_1 to X_2: $\{m \mid m : \mathbb{Z} \cdot X_1 \leq m \wedge m \leq X_2\}$
$S_1 \cup S_2$	**T-set** $\times$ **T-set** $\rightarrow$ **T-set**; union of S_1 and S_2: $\{s \mid s : T \cdot s \in S_1 \vee s \in S_2\}$
$S_1 - S_2$	**T-set** $\times$ **T-set** $\rightarrow$ **T-set**; difference of S_1 and S_2: $\{s \mid s : T \cdot s \in S_1 \wedge s \notin S_2\}$
$S_1 \cap S_2$	**T-set** $\times$ **T-set** $\rightarrow$ **T-set**; intersection of S_1 and S_2: $\{s \mid s : T \cdot s \in S_1 \wedge s \in S_2\}$
$\bigcup S$	**T-set-set** $\rightarrow$ **T-set**; distributed union of S: $\{s \mid s : T \cdot (\exists\ S' \in S \cdot s \in S')\}$
$\bigcap S$	**T-set-set** $\rightarrow$ **T-set**; distributed intersection of S: $\{s \mid s : T \cdot (\forall\ S' \in S \cdot s \in S')\}$
$E \in S$	$T \times$ **T-set** $\rightarrow \mathbb{B}$; E is an element of S
$E \notin S$	$T \times$ **T-set** $\rightarrow \mathbb{B}$; E is not an element of S
$S_1 \subseteq S_2$	**T-set** $\times$ **T-set** $\rightarrow \mathbb{B}$; S_1 is a subset of S_2 (possibly S_2 itself): $\forall\ s \in S_1 \cdot s \in S_2$
$S_1 \subset S_2$	**T-set** $\times$ **T-set** $\rightarrow \mathbb{B}$; S_1 is a proper subset of S_2 (not S_2 itself): $S_1 \subseteq S_2 \wedge S_1 \neq S_2$
card S	**T-set** $\rightarrow \mathbb{N}$; cardinality (number of elements) of S
$\mathcal{F} S$	**T-set** $\rightarrow$ **T-set-set**; finite power set of S, the set of finite subsets of S: $\{S' \mid S' :$ **T-set** $\cdot S' \subseteq S\}$
$S_1 = S_2$	**T-set** $\times$ **T-set** $\rightarrow \mathbb{B}$; equality: $S_1 \subseteq S_2 \wedge S_2 \subseteq S_1$
$S_1 \neq S_2$	**T-set** $\times$ **T-set** $\rightarrow \mathbb{B}$; inequality: $\neg\ (S_1 = S_2)$

5.3 Maps

5.3.1 Syntax

   map type expression = general map type expression
     | injective map type expression;

   general map type expression = type expression, '$\xrightarrow{m}$', type expression;

   injective map type expression =
     type expression, '$\xleftrightarrow{m}$', type expression;

   map expression = map enumeration | map comprehension;

   map enumeration = '{', maplet, {',', maplet}, '}' | '{', '↦', '}';

   maplet = expression, '↦', expression;

   map comprehension = '{', maplet, '|', bind list, ['·', expression], '}';

   map prefix operator = **'dom'** | **'rng'** | **'merge'**;

   map postfix operator = '-1';

   map infix operator = '∪' | '†' | '◁' | '◄' | '▷' | '▶' | '↑' | '∘';

   general infix operator = '=' | '≠';

   map application = expression, '(', expression, ')';

5.3.2 Meaning

A *map* M from a flat type T_1 (see section 5.8) to a type T_2 is a value that associates an element of T_2 with each element of T_1 (or of a subset of T_1). The set of elements of T_1 with which the map associates elements of T_2 is called the *domain* of the map, **dom** M. The domain may be empty, in which case the map is the *empty map*, denoted by {↦}. The set of elements of T_2 which the map associates with elements of T_1 is called the *range* of the map, **rng** M (**rng** M is defined only if all values in the range of M are flat, see section 5.8). The same element of the range can be associated with more than one element of the domain, but not vice versa. In VDM-SL the domain and range of a map are always finite. The element of the range associated with an element E of the domain is represented by a *map application* M(E) (so called because the map M is *applied* to the element E). Maps from T_1 to T_2 are members of the general map type $T_1 \xrightarrow{m} T_2$.

A map M of type $T_1 \xrightarrow{m} T_2$ may be thought of as represented by a collection of ordered pairs *mk*-(t_1, t_2), where t_2 is the element of T_2 associated

5.3 Compound Types – Maps

with the element t_1 of T_1; this is called the *graph* of the map, and can be defined as a set:

$$\{mk\text{-}(t_1, t_2) \mid t_1 \in \textbf{dom } M, t_2 \in \textbf{rng } M \cdot t_2 = M(t_1)\}$$

It is important to note however that a map in VDM-SL is not the same as its graph — a map is not a set and the set operators cannot be applied to it.

An *injective* map is one for which no element of the range is associated with more than one element of the domain. The injective map type $T_1 \xleftrightarrow{m} T_2$ is the same as the map type $T_1 \xrightarrow{m} T_2$ with an invariant:

$T_1 \xrightarrow{m} T_2$
$\textbf{inv } M \triangleq \forall m1, m2 \in \textbf{dom } M \cdot (M(m1) = M(m2)) \Rightarrow (m1 = m2)$

An injective map M has an *inverse map* M^{-1}: $M^{-1}(M(t)) = t$, provided that the elements of the range are all flat values (see section 5.8). The range and domain of M^{-1} are the domain and range, respectively, of M.

A *map enumeration* has the form:

$$\{E_1 \mapsto E_1', E_2 \mapsto E_2', ..., E_n \mapsto E_n'\}$$

where the E_i and the E_i' are expressions. It denotes the map which maps the value of E_1 to the value of E_1', the value of E_2 to the value of E_2', ..., the value of E_n to the value of E_n'.

For the value of a map enumeration to be defined, all the values of the E_i must be flat; and if any E_i, E_j have the same value then so must the corresponding E_i' and E_j'. Thus the following is invalid:

$$\{1 \mapsto 1, 2 \mapsto 3, 3 \mapsto 2, 2 \mapsto 1\}$$

The special map enumeration:

$$\{\mapsto\}$$

denotes the empty map, with empty domain and range; this is a value of every map type and injective map type, unless excluded by an invariant. The *maplet arrow* $\mapsto$ is included to distinguish the empty map from the empty set $\{\}$.

5.3 Compound Types – Maps

A *map comprehension* has one of the forms:

$\{E \mapsto E' \mid Bd_1, Bd_2, ..., Bd_n \cdot B\}$
$\{E \mapsto E' \mid Bd_1, Bd_2, ..., Bd_n\}$

where E and E´ are expressions, B is a Boolean expression, and each Bd_i is a set bind $Pt_i \in S$ or a type bind $Pt_i : T$ (see section 6.2). It denotes the map which maps each value of E to the corresponding value of E´, evaluated for each combination of bindings from $Bd_1, Bd_2, ..., Bd_n$ for which the value of the Boolean expression B is **true** (not **false** nor undefined). If B is not supplied, as in the second form, the default is **true**, and all combinations of bindings are taken.

The scope of any pattern identifiers in the binds Bd_i is the preceding maplet E ↦ E´ and the following Boolean expression B; if the same pattern identifier occurs more than once, only sets of bindings in which it is bound to the same value are considered. A more compact form of bind list is available when a set or type is repeated; see section 6.2. For the value of a map comprehension to be defined, all combinations of bindings must give flat values for E, and if any two choices of bindings give the same value for E, then they must also give the same value for E´. Thus the following is invalid:

$\{x + y \mapsto x \times y \mid x \in \{2,3\}, y \in \{1,2\}\}$

Operators on maps are as follows.

- A *map merge* has the form:

    $M_1 \cup M_2$

    where M_1 and M_2 are two *compatible* maps, that is, any common element of **dom** M_1 and **dom** M_2 is mapped to the same value by both maps. It combines the two maps M_1 and M_2 so that the result maps the elements of **dom** M_1 as does M_1, and the elements of **dom** M_2 as does M_2.

    Merging is commutative and associative, and so can be extended unambiguously to any number of maps. The graph of $M_1 \cup M_2$ is the union of the graphs of M_1 and M_2, which accounts for the use of the union symbol, but this can be misleading: unlike set union, map merge cannot be applied to any two arbitrary maps.

5.3 Compound Types – Maps

- A set S of compatible maps can be merged by a *distributed merge* with the form:

    merge S

- A *map override* has the form:

    M$_1$ † M$_2$

    where M$_1$ and M$_2$ are two maps. It is like a map merge except that M$_1$ and M$_2$ need not be compatible; any common elements are mapped as by M$_2$ (so M$_2$ overrides M$_1$). Thus map overriding is not commutative (though it is associative) and no distributed operator is provided. If M$_1$ and M$_2$ are compatible, then M$_1$ † M$_2$ = M$_1$ ∪ M$_2$.

- Two maps M$_1$ and M$_2$ may, subject to certain constraints, be *composed* to give a composite map by a *map composition*. This has the form:

    M$_1$ ∘ M$_2$

    Its value is a map with the same domain as M$_2$; the element associated with an element E is found by first applying map M$_2$ and then applying map M$_1$ to the result:

    (M$_1$ ∘ M$_2$)(E) = M$_1$(M$_2$(E))

    This is defined only if M$_1$ can be applied to each M$_2$(E), so that the range of M$_2$ is a subset of the domain of M$_1$. The order of applying the maps is consistent with the syntax of map application, from right to left. Map composition is not commutative, in general, but it is associative.

- A map can be composed with itself, provided that its range is a subset of its domain. Repeated composition of a map M with itself is called *map iteration*, and is denoted in the same way as numeric exponentiation; as composition is associative, there is no ambiguity:

    M ↑ N

    where N is an integer expression with a nonnegative value. As with exponentiation, the meaning of map iteration can be extended to the cases where N = 0 or 1: for N = 0 the result is the *identity map*,

5.3 Compound Types – Maps

which maps each element of the domain of M to itself: for N = 1 the result is just the map M. These special cases apply to any map M.

- There are four *map restriction operators* for producing maps defining the same association as M but with restricted domain or range. They each take a map M and a set S, and the result is the submap of M with domain or range restricted by including only those elements which are also elements of S, or by excluding those elements which are also elements of S. All four combinations are catered for:

    S ◁ M   map M with domain restricted to elements of S
    S ⩤ M   map M with domain restricted by excluding elements of S
    M ▷ S   map M with range restricted to elements of S
    M ⩥ S   map M with range restricted by excluding elements of S

As a mnemonic device the domain operand is on the left and the range operand is on the right, in each case pointed at by the symbol, regarded as an arrow head; also the exclusion operator symbols include a minus sign.

- *Equality* and *inequality* of maps M_1 and M_2 are also available:

    $M_1 = M_2$ $M_1 \neq M_2$

$M_1 = M_2$ is **true** if M_1 and M_2 have the same domain and the same range, and map each element of the domain to the same element of the range, and is **false** otherwise. $M_1 \neq M_2$ is **false** if $M_1 = M_2$ is **true** and vice versa. M_1 and M_2 must be flat (see section 5.8).

- The element of the range of a map corresponding to an element of its domain is accessed by a *map application*, which is an application with the restricted form:

    M(E)

where M is a map expression and the E is an expression with a value that is an element of M's domain. The value of the map application is the element of M's range corresponding to E.

Map expressions are summarized in Tables 13 and 14.

5.3 Compound Types – Maps

5.3.3 Examples

Maps are useful in many situations. They are a natural model for any information base where entries are accessed by some kind of fixed key, for example a telephone directory:

directory = *name* $\xrightarrow{m}$ *entry*

They are useful also for maintaining a separate identity for objects irrespective of their contents: a database whose objects are accessed by navigation only could usefully be modelled by a map:

object-base : *object-id* $\xrightarrow{m}$ *object-body*

even though *object-id* values have no actual existence.

Examples of maps and map operators are provided by the vending machine specification of Appendix C.1. The maps *PRICES* and *INGREDIENTS* give the price of each drink and the ingredients needed to make it. The domain of both is the set of available drinks. The range of *PRICES* is the set of actual prices, and the range of *INGREDIENTS* is the set of sets of ingredients actually used.

The map *PRICES* is unlikely to be injective, as there will usually be different drinks with the same price. On the other hand *INGREDIENTS* probably is injective (appearances notwithstanding); *INGREDIENTS*$^{-1}$ maps sets of ingredients to the drinks they make.

The map *PRICES* could be defined as:

{*d* ↦ *m* | *d* : *Drink*, *m* : *Money*, ·
 m = *sum*({*COSTS*(*I*) | *I* ∈ *INGREDIENTS*(*d*)}) + *profit*

If *F-COSTS* = {TEA ↦ 5, COFFEE ↦ 5, CHOCOLATE ↦ 6} and *A-COSTS* = {MILK ↦ 2, SUGAR ↦ 1, WATER ↦ 0}, then *F-COSTS* ∪ *A-COSTS* = *COSTS*.

If *PREF* : *Person* $\xrightarrow{m}$ *Drink* maps a set of people to their preferred drinks, then *PRICES* ∘ *PREF* shows how much each person should contribute to a round of drinks.

5.3 Compound Types – Maps

If $Cash : Coin \xrightarrow{m} \mathbb{N}$ is a map showing the number of each denomination of coin held (see Appendix C.1) then $\{ONE, TWO\} \triangleleft Cash$ and $\{ONE, TWO\} \triangleleft Cash$ show the holdings of copper and silver respectively; $Cash \triangleright \{0\}$ and $Cash \triangleright \{0\}$ show the coins not held (all mapped to 0) and the coins held, respectively. If $c \in \textbf{dom}\ (Cash \triangleright \{0\})$ then $Cash(c) = 0$.

For an example of map iteration, let $cycle : \textbf{char}^+ \xrightarrow{m} \textbf{char}^+$ be a map that cyclically shifts a set of words one place left. Then (assuming "$STRIPE$" $\in \textbf{dom}\ cycle$):

$cycle \uparrow 0\ ("STRIPE") = "STRIPE"$
$cycle \uparrow 1\ ("STRIPE") = "TRIPES"$
$cycle \uparrow 2\ ("STRIPE") = "RIPEST"$ etc.

A distributed map override operator for a sequence of maps of the same type, in which each element of the sequence overrides all previous elements, can be defined by a polymorphic function definition as follows (for sequences, and the operators **elems, inds,** and **len** see section 5.4).

$dover : (@T1 \xrightarrow{m} @T2)^* \rightarrow @T1 \xrightarrow{m} @T2$
$dover(S) \triangleq$
  $\{t1 \mapsto t2\ |\ t1 \in \bigcup \{\textbf{dom}\ M\ |\ M \in \textbf{elems}\ S\ \}\ \cdot$
    $\exists i \in \textbf{inds}\ S \cdot (t1 \in \textbf{dom}\ S(i)) \land (t2 = S(i)(t1)) \land$
    $((i = \textbf{len}\ S) \lor$
    $(t1 \notin \bigcup \{\textbf{dom}\ M\ |\ M \in \textbf{elems}\ S\ (i+1,...,\textbf{len}\ S\ )\}))\}$

Alternatively, *dover* could be defined recursively by

$dover : (@T1 \xrightarrow{m} @T2)^* \rightarrow @T1 \xrightarrow{m} @T2$
$dover(S) \triangleq$
  if len $S = 0$ **then** $\{\ \}$ **else** $dover\ (S\ (1,...,\textbf{len}\ S\ -1))\ \dagger\ S\ (\textbf{len}\ S\ )$

In the vending machine specification in Appendix C.1, maps are used for fixed values, giving the value of each denomination of coin and the ingredients of each kind of drink; and for variable values, such as the number of each kind of coin held. This last is an example of a *multiset* or *bag*, which is similar to a set but can contain the same element more than once. Multisets are not supported as such by VDM-SL, but can easily be

5.3 Compound Types – Maps

modelled by maps from each possible element to the number of times it appears. It is usual to restrict the domain to elements appearing at least once, so that for example a multiset of real numbers would be represented as a map of type $\mathbb{R} \xrightarrow{m} \mathbb{N}_1$.

Section 7.5 defines some polymorphic functions for operating on multisets, and shows how they can be used to simplify the vending machine specification.

5.3 Compound Types – Maps

Table 13 Map operators and expressions: map operators

operator	signature & value
dom M	$(T_1 \xrightarrow{m} T_2) \to T_1\text{-}\mathbf{set}$; domain of M
rng M	$(T_1 \xrightarrow{m} T_2) \to T_2\text{-}\mathbf{set}$; range of M; T_2 must be flat
M^{-1}	$(T_1 \xrightarrow{m} T_2) \to (T_2 \xrightarrow{m} T_1)$; map inversion: $\{t_2 \mapsto t_1 \mid t_1 : T_1, t_2 : T_2$ $\cdot\ t_1 \in \mathbf{dom}\ M \land t_2 = M(t_1)\}$; M must be injective and T_2 flat
$M_1 \cup M_2$	$(T_1 \xrightarrow{m} T_2) \times (T_1 \xrightarrow{m} T_2) \to (T_1 \xrightarrow{m} T_2)$; map merge: $\{t_1 \mapsto t_2 \mid t_1 : T_1, t_2 : T_2 \cdot (t_1 \in \mathbf{dom}\ M_1 \land t_2 = M_1(t_1)) \lor (t_1 \in \mathbf{dom}\ M_2 \land t_2 = M_2(t_1))\}$; M_1, M_2 must be compatible
merge S	$(T_1 \xrightarrow{m} T_2)\text{-}\mathbf{set} \to (T_1 \xrightarrow{m} T_2)$; distributed merge: $\{t_1 \mapsto t_2 \mid t_1 : T_1, t_2 : T_2 \cdot (\exists M \in S \cdot t_1 \in \mathbf{dom}\ M \land t_2 = M(t_1))\}$; the elements of S must be compatible
$M_1 \dagger M_2$	$(T_1 \xrightarrow{m} T_2) \times (T_1 \xrightarrow{m} T_2) \to (T_1 \xrightarrow{m} T_2)$; map override: $\{t_1 \mapsto t_2 \mid t_1 : T_1, t_2 : T_2 \cdot (t_1 \in (\mathbf{dom}\ M_1 - \mathbf{dom}\ M_2) \land t_2 = M_1(t_1)) \lor (t_1 \in \mathbf{dom}\ M_2 \land t_2 = M_2(t_1)) \}$
$S \triangleleft M$	$(T_1\text{-}\mathbf{set}) \times (T_1 \xrightarrow{m} T_2) \to (T_1 \xrightarrow{m} T_2)$; domain restrict to: $\{t_1 \mapsto t_2 \mid t_1 \in S \cap \mathbf{dom}\ M,\ t_2 : T_2 \cdot t_2 = M(t_1)\}$
$S \triangleleft M$	$(T_1\text{-}\mathbf{set}) \times (T_1 \xrightarrow{m} T_2) \to (T_1 \xrightarrow{m} T_2)$; domain restrict by: $\{t_1 \mapsto t_2 \mid t_1 \in (\mathbf{dom}\ M - S),\ t_2 : T_2 \cdot t_2 = M(t_1)\}$
$M \triangleright S$	$(T_1 \xrightarrow{m} T_2) \times (T_2\text{-}\mathbf{set}) \to (T_1 \xrightarrow{m} T_2)$; restrict to range: $\{t_1 \mapsto t_2 \mid t_1 \in \mathbf{dom}\ M,\ t_2 \in S \cap \mathbf{rng}\ M \cdot t_2 = M(t_1)\}$
$M \triangleright S$	$(T_1 \xrightarrow{m} T_2) \times (T_2\text{-}\mathbf{set}) \to (T_1 \xrightarrow{m} T_2)$; range restrict by: $\{t_1 \mapsto t_2 \mid t_1 \in \mathbf{dom}\ M,\ t_2 \in (\mathbf{rng}\ M - S) \cdot t_2 = M(t_1)\}$
$M_1 \circ M_2$	$(T_2 \xrightarrow{m} T_3) \times (T_1 \xrightarrow{m} T_2) \to (T_1 \xrightarrow{m} T_3)$; map composition: $\{t \mapsto M_1(M_2(t)) \mid t \in \mathbf{dom}\ M_2\}$; needs $\mathbf{rng}\ M_2 \subseteq \mathbf{dom}\ M_1$.
$M \uparrow N$	$(T \xrightarrow{m} T) \times \mathbb{N} \to (T \xrightarrow{m} T)$; map iteration: $N = 0$: identity map $\{t \mapsto t \mid t \in \mathbf{dom}\ M\}$; $N = 1$: M; $N \geq 2$: $M \circ M \circ \ldots \circ M$, needs $\mathbf{rng}\ M \subseteq \mathbf{dom}\ M$
$M_1 = M_2$	$(T_1 \xrightarrow{m} T_2) \times (T_1 \xrightarrow{m} T_2) \to \mathbb{B}$; equality: $\mathbf{dom}\ M_1 = \mathbf{dom}\ M_2 \land \forall t \in \mathbf{dom}\ M_1 \cdot M_1(t) = M_2(t)$
$M_1 \neq M_2$	$(T_1 \xrightarrow{m} T_2) \times (T_1 \xrightarrow{m} T_2) \to \mathbb{B}$; inequality: $\neg\ M_1 = M_2$

5.3 Compound Types – Maps

Table 14 Map operators and expressions: map constructors and applications

operator	signature & value
$\{E_1 \mapsto E_1',...,E_n \mapsto E_n'\}$	$(T_1 \times T_2) \times ... \times (T_1 \times T_2) \rightarrow (T_1 \xrightarrow{m} T_2)$; map enumeration: maps each E_i to E_i'. All $\{E_i \mapsto E_i'\}$ must be compatible; all E_i must be flat
$\{ \mapsto \}$	$() \rightarrow (T_1 \xrightarrow{m} T_2)$; special map enumeration: the empty map
$\{E \mapsto E' \mid Bd_1,...,Bd_n \cdot B\}$	$(T_1 \times T_2) \times \mathbb{B} \rightarrow (T_1 \xrightarrow{m} T_2)$; map comprehension: maps E to E′ for each set of bindings from the Bd_i satisfying B. All $\{E \mapsto E'\}$ must be compatible, all E must be flat
$\{E \mapsto E' \mid Bd_1,...,Bd_n\}$	$(T_1 \times T_2) \rightarrow (T_1 \xrightarrow{m} T_2)$; map comprehension: same as $\{E \mapsto E' \mid Bd_1, ..., Bd_n \cdot \textbf{true}\}$
M(E)	$(T_1 \xrightarrow{m} T_2) \times T_1 \rightarrow T_2$; map application: the element of **rng** M associated with E. Must have $E \in \textbf{dom } M$

5.4 Sequences

5.4.1 Syntax

    sequence type expression = general sequence type expression | nonempty sequence type expression;

    general sequence type expression = type expression, '*';

    nonempty sequence type expression = type expression, '+';

    sequence expression = sequence enumeration | sequence comprehension | subsequence expression | sequence modification;

    sequence enumeration = '[', [expression list], ']';

    sequence comprehension = '[', expression, '|', set bind, ['·', expression], ']';

    subsequence expression = expression, '(', expression, ',', '...', ',', expression, ')';

    sequence modification = expression, '†', '{', sequence modifier, {',', sequence modifier}, '}';

    sequence modifier = expression, '↦', expression;

    expression list = expression, {',', expression};

    sequence prefix operator = 'hd' | 'tl' | 'len' | 'elems' | 'inds' | 'conc';

    sequence infix operator = '⌢';

    general infix operator = '=' | '≠';

    sequence application = expression, '(', expression, ')';

5.4.2 Meaning

A *sequence* is an ordered set of elements, indexed 1, 2, ..., n; all sequences in VDM-SL are finite. A sequence can be regarded as represented by a map from an initial segment of the positive integers to the sequence value, but this analogy must not be pushed too far: the map operators do not apply to sequences. A sequence may be empty.

A *sequence type* is the type of finite sequences of elements of a type, either including the empty sequence (general sequence type) or excluding it (nonempty sequence type). The nonempty sequence type T^+ is equivalent to the general sequence type T^* with an invariant:

65

5.4 Compound Types – Sequences

$$T^+ = T^* \text{ inv } Q \triangleq \text{len } Q > 0$$

A *sequence enumeration* has the form:

[E_1, E_2, ..., E_n]

where E_1, E_2, ..., E_n are expressions; it denotes the sequence value comprising the values of E_1, E_2, ..., E_n in that order.

The special sequence enumeration:

[ ]

denotes the *empty sequence*, with no elements. It is an element of every general sequence type, unless excluded by an invariant.

A *sequence comprehension* has one of the forms:

[E | Id $\in$ S · B]
[E | Id $\in$ S]

where E is an expression, S is a ℝ-**set** expression, and B is a Boolean expression. Note that the set bind is restricted to this simple form with an identifier rather than a general pattern. The sequence comprehension denotes the sequence consisting of the values of E evaluated for Id bound to each element of S for which B is **true** (not **false** nor undefined), in order of increasing value of Id. The scope of the identifier Id is the expressions E and (if present) B.

If B is absent, as in the second case, it is taken to be **true**, and all elements of S contribute, so that **len** [E | Id $\in$ S] = **card** S. Thus:

[$n \uparrow 2$ | $n \in \{1,...,5\}$]

is the sequence of squares [1,4,9,16,25], while:

[$n \uparrow 2$ | $n \in \{1,...,5\}$ · n **mod** 2 = 1]

is the sequence [1,9,25]. As another example, a sequence S reversed is:

[S(**len** S +1−i) | $i \in$ **inds** S]

5.4 Compound Types – Sequences

A *subsequence* of a sequence Q is a sequence formed from consecutive elements of Q. It may be denoted by a *subsequence expression* with the form:

$Q(X_1, ..., X_2)$

where X_1 and X_2 are numeric expressions (normally positive integers within the index range of Q). It denotes the subsequence of Q consisting of all elements $Q(i)$ for which $X_1 \leq i \leq X_2$. Here the commas and dots are symbols of VDM-SL, not part of the notation. If $X_1 > X_2$, the subsequence expression represents the empty sequence.

Operators on sequences are as follows.

- Corresponding to map override is the *sequence modification* with the form:

    $Q \dagger \{N_1 \mapsto E_1, N_2 \mapsto E_2, ..., N_n \mapsto E_n\}$

    where Q is a sequence, the N_i are expressions whose values are positive integers, and the E_i are expressions. The indices N_i must all lie within the index range of Q; and the maps $\{N_i \mapsto E_i\}$ must all be compatible. This takes the sequence Q and replaces the N_1th element by the value of E_1, the N_2th element by the value of E_2, ..., and the N_nth element by the value of E_n.

- Corresponding to map merge is *sequence concatenation*, with the form:

    $Q_1 \frown Q_2$

    where Q_1 and Q_2 are sequences. This is the sequence consisting of the elements of Q_1 followed by those of Q_2, in order.

- Concatenation is associative, and *distributed concatenation* is available; this operates on a sequence Q of sequences, and concatenates them all together in order:

    conc Q

    This is $Q(1) \frown Q(2) \frown ... \frown Q(n)$, where $n = $ **len** Q.

5.4 Compound Types – Sequences

- The *head* and *tail* operators are:

    hd Q   **tl** Q

    hd Q is the first component of Q, and **tl** Q is the sequence Q with its head removed. Note that the head is an element of Q, while the tail is a subsequence of Q: Q = [**hd** Q] ⁀ **tl** Q. The head and tail are undefined if Q is empty.

- The *length* operator:

    len Q

    This is the number of elements of Q (a non-negative integer).

- The *elements* operator and the *indices* operator:

    elems Q   **inds** Q

    These are respectively the components of Q, as a set of type T-**set**, and the indices of Q, as a set of positive integers. **elems** Q is defined only if all elements of Q are flat values.

- *Equality* and *inequality* are available for sequences of all flat types:

    $Q_1 = Q_2$ $Q_1 \neq Q_2$

    where Q_1 and Q_2 are sequences of the same type. $Q_1 = Q_2$ is **true** if Q_1 and Q_2 have the same length, and every component of Q_1 is equal to the corresponding component of Q_2, and **false** otherwise. $Q_1 \neq Q_2$ is **true** if $Q_1 = Q_2$ is **false** and vice versa.

- A component of a sequence can be accessed by a *sequence application*. This has the form:

    Q(N)

    where Q is a non-empty sequence and N is a positive integer within the index range of the sequence Q. The value of the application is the element of the sequence with index N. The first element of a sequence has index 1, so **hd** Q = Q(1), and **tl** Q = Q(2,...,**len** Q).

Sequence expressions are summarized in Table 15.

5.4 Compound Types – Sequences

5.4.3 Examples

Sequences are useful whenever an ordered set of items is to be specified. Strings of characters are a very common example, see section 4.4. For another example, if a telephone directory represented as a map of names to entries is to be printed in alphabetical order, the names could be ordered as a sequence of type $name^+$. The alphabetical ordering to be used could be defined as a Boolean function on pairs of strings, since it is unlikely to be purely lexicographic; but the basic lexicographic ordering could be defined as a sequence of type $char^+$ containing each character once only.

The names of the planets known in antiquity, in order outwards from the Sun, is the sequence *planets*:

["*Mercury*", "*Venus*", "*Earth*", "*Mars*", "*Jupiter*", "*Saturn*"]

Each element of *planets* is itself a sequence of characters: "*Mercury*" represents ['M', 'e', 'r', 'c', 'u', 'r', 'y'] (see section 4.4). The distributed concatenation **conc** *planets* is the string:

"*MercuryVenusEarthMarsJupiterSaturn*".

The subsequence:

planets(1,...,2)

is the sequence of inferior planets (within Earth's orbit). Our home planet can be renamed more in context by the sequence modification:

planets † {3 ↦ "*Tellus*"}

The sequence of planets can be brought up to date by concatenating recent discoveries:

planets ⁀ ["*Uranus*", "*Neptune*", "*Pluto*"]

The head **hd** *planets* = "*Mercury*", the tail **tl** (*planets*(3)) = "*arth*". **len** *planets* = 6; **len** "*Mercury*" = 7. **elems** *planets* is:

{"*Earth*", "*Jupiter*", "*Mars*", "*Mercury*", "*Saturn*", "*Venus*"}

and **inds** *planets* = {1,...,6}.

5.4 Compound Types – Sequences

Sequences can also be used as generalizations of sets (*multisets* or *bags*) which allow repeated elements, but with no implied order. However this is overspecifying, and it is better to define a type with the properties required and no others (see section 5.3.3).

An example of a naturally ordered set of items is a sequence of events in time. For instance if the vending machine specified in Appendix C.1 were enhanced to keep a log of all drinks dispensed, this could be represented as a sequence:

$$LOG : Drink^*$$

initialized to [ ] and updated by a term in the postcondition:

$$LOG = LOG^{\leftarrow} \frown [result]$$

5.4 Compound Types – Sequences

Table 15 Sequence operators and expressions

expression	signature & value
$[E_1,...,E_n]$	$T \times ... \times T \rightarrow T^*$; sequence enumeration: the sequence comprising the values of $E_1, ..., E_n$ in order
$[\,]$	$(\,) \rightarrow T^*$; sequence enumeration: the empty sequence
$[E \mid Id \in S \cdot B]$	$T \times R\text{-set} \times B \rightarrow T^*$; sequence comprehension: the sequence of values of E satisfying B for Id bound to each element of S in increasing order
$[E \mid Id \in S]$	$T \times R\text{-set} \rightarrow T^*$; sequence comprehension: same as $[E \mid Id \in S \cdot \mathbf{true}]$
$Q(X_1, ..., X_2)$	$T^* \times R \times R \rightarrow T^*$; subsequence: if $X_1 \le X_2$, the sequence $[Q(n) \mid X_1 \le n \wedge n \le X_2]$; else $[\,]$
$Q^\dagger \{N_1 \mapsto E_1, ...\}$	$T^* \times (N_1 \times T) \times ... \rightarrow T^*$; sequence modification: sequence Q with element $Q(N_1)$ replaced by E_1, etc. The $\{N_i \mapsto E_i\}$ must be compatible
hd Q	$T^+ \rightarrow T$; sequence head: $Q(1)$, undefined if $Q = [\,]$
tl Q	$T^+ \rightarrow T^*$; sequence tail: $[Q(2), ..., Q(n)]$, where $n = \mathbf{len}\ Q$; undefined if $Q = [\,]$
len Q	$T^* \rightarrow N$; sequence length: number of components of Q
elems Q	$T^* \rightarrow T\text{-set}$; sequence elements: the set of components of Q: $\{Q(i) \mid i \in \mathbf{len}\ Q\}$. The components of Q must all be flat
inds Q	$T^* \rightarrow N_1\text{-set}$; sequence indices: the set of indices of Q: $\{1, ..., \mathbf{len}\ Q\}$
conc Q	$T^{**} \rightarrow T^*$; distributed sequence concatenation: if $Q = [\,], [\,]$; otherwise $Q(1) \frown ... \frown Q(\mathbf{len}\ Q)$
$Q_1 \frown Q_2$	$T^* \times T^* \rightarrow T^*$; sequence concatenation: $[Q_1(1), ..., Q_1(\mathbf{len}\ Q_1), Q_2(1), ..., Q_2(\mathbf{len}\ Q_2)]$
$Q_1 = Q_2$	$T^* \times T^* \rightarrow B$; equality: $\mathbf{len}\ Q_1 = \mathbf{len}\ Q_2 \wedge \forall n \in \mathbf{inds}\ Q_1 \cdot Q_1(n) = Q_2(n)$; Q_1, Q_2 must be flat
$Q_1 \ne Q_2$	$T^* \times T^* \rightarrow B$; inequality: $\neg\ Q_1 = Q_2$
$Q(N)$	$T^* \times N_1 \rightarrow T$; sequence application: Nth element of Q

5.5 Composite values (records)

5.5.1 Syntax

   composite type expression = **'compose'**, identifier, **'of'**, field list, **'end'**;

   field list = {field};

   field = [identifier, ':'], type expression;

   type definition = ... | identifier, '::', field list, [invariant definition] | ...;

   record expression = record construction | record modification;

   record construction = identifier, '(', expression list, ')';

   record modification = 'µ', '(', expression, ',', record modifier, {',', record modifier}, ')';

   record modifier = identifier, '↦', expression;

   field selection = expression, '.', identifier;

   general infix operator = '=' | '≠';

5.5.2 Meaning

A *record* or *composite value* is a collection of component values or *fields*; the fields may have associated identifiers by which they can be referred to.

A *composite type expression* has the form:

    compose Id **of**   or   **compose** Id **of**
       $Id_1 : T_1$ T_1
       $Id_2 : T_2$ T_2
       ...   ...
       $Id_n : T_n$ T_n
    end   **end**

where Id and the Id_i are identifiers and the T_i are type expressions. It denotes the type of records with fields having names Id_i (in the form on the left) and types T_i respectively. All the fields may be anonymous, as in the form on the right, and cannot then be referred to by field selections. The identifier Id is called the *tag* of the type; it used to allow the declaration of different composite types with the same fields. This gives the effect of *name equivalence* for composite types; all other types have

5.5 Compound Types – Composite values (records)

structural equivalence. It is possible to have no fields, in which case the record type contains a single value.

The tag identifier Id is not declared, and is not itself usable. However, the two identifiers *mk*-Id and *is*-Id are implicitly declared by the composite type expression, with global scope, for use in record constructions (see below) and type membership expressions (see section 3.2) respectively. The field identifiers Id$_i$ are also declared with global scope, but can be used only in a field selection or a record modification, when the record type is implicitly identified. The field identifiers are therefore overloadable: they may be freely used elsewhere, but all the field identifiers in a single composite type expression must be different.

There is a special form of type definition for composite types (see section 3.2):

```
Id :: Id₁ : T₁        or   Id :: T₁
      Id₂ : T₂                  T₂
      ...                       ...
      Idₙ : Tₙ                  Tₙ
```

This stands for

```
Id = compose Id of    or   Id = compose Id of
      Id₁ : T₁                    T₁
      Id₂ : T₂                    T₂
      ...                         ...
      Idₙ : Tₙ                    Tₙ
     end                         end
```

where the same identifier Id is used for the tag and the name of the type. These identifiers can be different in an explicit composite type definition: the type name is used for all references to the type. This form of type definition declares both the type name Id and the identifiers *mk*-Id and *is*-Id, all with global scope, as well as the field identifiers Id$_i$ as described above.

A *record construction* has the form:

   mk-Id(E$_1$, E$_2$, ..., E$_n$)

where Id is the tag of a composite type and the E$_i$ are expressions of the field types of R. There must be one expression E$_i$ for each field of the record type R; it must have a value of the type T$_i$ of the field. The identifier *mk*-Id is implicitly defined for each composite type; only those

73

5.5 Compound Types – Composite values (records)

identifiers may be used to form record constructions. The identifier *mk-Id* is also used to form a record pattern of type Id, see section 6.2. The record construction denotes the record value of type with tag Id whose fields are the expressions E_i in order.

A *record modification* has the form:

$$\mu(R, Id_1 \mapsto E_1, Id_2 \mapsto E_2, ..., Id_n \mapsto E_n)$$

where R is a record expression, the Id_i are distinct field identifiers of the type of R, and the E_i are expressions of the corresponding field types. It denotes the record value which is the same as R except that the fields with identifiers Id_i have values E_i respectively.

The only operators for record types are *equality* and *inequality*, for two records of the same type:

$$Q_1 = Q_2 \qquad\qquad Q_1 \neq Q_2$$

$Q_1 = Q_2$ is **true** if the corresponding fields of Q_1 and Q_2 are equal, and is **false** otherwise. $Q_1 \neq Q_2$ is **true** if $Q_1 = Q_2$ is **false** and vice versa. All the fields of Q_1 and Q_2 must have flat values.

A *field selection* has the form:

R . Id

where R is a record value, and Id is the identifier of a field within R's record type. It denotes the value of the field with fieldname Id in the record value R.

5.5.3 Examples

As an example of record types, polar and Cartesian coordinate types can be defined as:

Coord-1 = **compose** *Polar* **of**
    ARG : $\mathbb{R}$
    MOD : $\mathbb{R}$
end
inv *mk-Polar*(r, θ) $\underline{\triangle}$ (r ≥ 0) ∧ (0 ≤ θ) ∧ (θ < 2 × π)

5.5 Compound Types – Composite values (records)

 Coord-2 = **compose** *Cartesian* **of**
  x : $\mathbb{R}$
  y : $\mathbb{R}$
 end

By sacrificing the separate type names *Coord-1* and *Coord-2*, the coordinate type definitions above could be rewritten as:

 Polar :: *ARG* : $\mathbb{R}$
    MOD : $\mathbb{R}$
 inv *mk-Polar*(r, θ) ≙ (r ≥ 0) ∧ (0 ≤ θ) ∧ (θ < 2 × π)

 Cartesian :: *x* : $\mathbb{R}$
     y : $\mathbb{R}$

With these coordinate types, *mk-Polar*(1, π/2) and *mk-Cartesian*(0, 1) represent the same point. The type definition of *Polar* also illustrates the use of *mk-Polar* to form a record pattern, in the invariant.

To illustrate record modification, the function:

 rot(*c* : *Coord-1*, ϕ : $\mathbb{R}$) ≙
  μ(*c*, *MOD* → *c.MOD* + ϕ − 2 × π × **floor**((*c.MOD* + ϕ)/(2 × π)))

rotates a point through an angle ϕ about the origin (the last term is to preserve the invariant).

Records are useful whenever disparate items of data are to be treated together. For instance a telephone directory entry (indexed by name) might consist of an address and telephone number:

 Entry :: *ADDRESS* : **char**$^+$
    NUMBER : $\mathbb{N}_1$

The address and number of an entry *this-entry* are accessed by field selections: *this-entry.ADDRESS*, *this-entry.NUMBER*. Updating an entry is represented by record modification, for example changing the number: μ(*this-entry*, *NUMBER* ↦ *new-number*). A new entry is represented by a record construction: *mk-entry*("T.McMillan", 276791).

5.5 Compound Types – Composite values (records)

Record types can be nested. For instance an entry could be one field of a personnel record:

    Record ::   *NAME* : *Name*
                  ENTRY : *Entry*

so that the address for a record *r* is *r.ENTRY.ADDRESS*.

An invariant can be used to enforce relationships between the fields of record values. For instance a 20th century date in the Gregorian calendar can be represented (see section 6.5 for cases expressions) as a record of type:

    Date :: *DAY* : $\mathbb{N}_1$
              MONTH : $\mathbb{N}_1$
              YEAR : $\mathbb{N}_1$
    inv (*mk-Date*(*d*, *m*, *y*) ≜
      (1901 ≤ *y*) ∧ (*y* ≤ 2000) ∧
      (*m* ≤ 12) ∧
      (*d* ≤
      cases *m* :
        9, 4, 6, 11 → 30,
        2 → **if** ((*y* **rem** 4 = 0) ∧ (*y* **rem** 100 ≠ 0))
               ∨ (*y* **rem** 400 = 0) **then** 29 **else** 28,
        others → 31
      end)

A record can sometimes be used as a refinement of a map, by including the domain elements as a field; this may be closer to a data structure supported by the implementation language. This is particularly convenient when the domain of the map has no obvious representation as a set of integers (when a sequence may be more suitable). For example, suppose in a further refinement of the vending machine specification of Appendix C.1 the type *Drink* was refined to an explicit set SWEET-WHITE-TEA, UNSWEETENED-BLACK-COFFEE, and so on (perhaps corresponding to push-buttons on the machine). Then the map *INGREDIENTS* could be refined to a record:

5.5 Compound Types – Composite values (records)

```
INGREDIENTS :: DRINK     : Drink
               CHOCOLATE : B
               TEA       : B
               COFFEE    : B
               SUGAR     : B
               MILK      : B
```

A record type with no fields is sometimes useful for consistency when a class of record types is specified which in general have one or more fields but in some cases have none. For example, in the abstract syntax of VDM-SL literals, there could be a record type for each type of literal:

Literal = BoolLit | RealLit | ... | NilLit

BoolLit :: val : B

RealLit :: val : R

...

NilLit ::

There would be only one value of type NilLit, namely mk-NilLit ( ).

Table 16 Composite value operators and expressions

expression	signature & value
mk-$T(E_1, ..., E_n)$	$T_1 \times ... \times T_n \rightarrow T$; record construction: the record of type with tag T, with fields E_i
$\mu(R, Id_1 \mapsto E_1, ..., Id_m \mapsto E_m)$	$T \times T_1 \times ... \times T_m \rightarrow T$; record modification: R with values E_i for fields Id_i, other fields unchanged
R . Id	$T \rightarrow T_i$; field selection: the value of field Id of record R
$R_1 = R_2$	$T \times T \rightarrow B$; equality: R_1 . Id = R_2 . Id for all fields Id. R_1 and R_2 must be flat
$R_1 \neq R_2$	$T \times T \rightarrow B$; inequality: $\neg(R_1 = R_2)$

5.6 Compound Types – Product values (tuples)

5.6 Product values (tuples)

5.6.1 Syntax

   product type expression = type expression, '×', type expression;

   tuple expression = tuple construction;

   tuple construction = 'mk-', '(', expression list, ')';

   general infix operator = '=' | '≠';

5.6.2 Meaning

A *tuple* is an ordered set of 2 or more values, called its *components*. A *product type* expression has the form:

   $T_1 \times T_2 \times ... \times T_n$

where the T_i are type expressions, and $n \geq 2$; it denotes the set of tuples with components t_1 from type T_1, t_2 from type T_2, ..., and t_n from T_n. This is not the same as the composite type:

   compose Id **of** $T_1, T_2, ..., T_n$

for the latter identifies a unique type, tagged by the identifier Id, whereas the former does not. To put it another way, if Id_1 and Id_2 are different identifiers, then in:

   $Id_1 = T_1 \times T_2 \times ... \times T_n$
   $Id_2 = T_1 \times T_2 \times ... \times T_n$

Id_1 and Id_2 denote the same type, whereas in:

   $Id_1 :: T_1, T_2, ..., T_n$
   $Id_2 :: T_1, T_2, ..., T_n$

they denote different types.

The type operator × is not associative: $T_1 \times (T_2 \times T_3)$ and $(T_1 \times T_2) \times T_3$ are not the same, though the distinction is not usually important. × has no association, so that $T_1 \times T_2 \times T_3$ is different to both $T_1 \times (T_2 \times T_3)$ and $(T_1 \times T_2) \times T_3$. If t_1, t_2, and t_3 are members of types T_1, T_2, and T_3

5.6 Compound Types – Product values (tuples)

respectively, then typical members of $T_1 \times T_2 \times T_3$, $T_1 \times (T_2 \times T_3)$, and $(T_1 \times T_2) \times T_3$ are the values of the tuple constructions $mk\text{-}(t_1, t_2, t_3)$, $mk\text{-}(t_1, mk\text{-}(t_2, t_3))$, and $mk\text{-}(mk\text{-}(t_1, t_2), t_3)$ respectively. It is also not commutative; unless T_1 is the same type as T_2, $T_1 \times T_2$ and $T_2 \times T_1$ denote different types.

A *tuple construction* has the form:

$mk\text{-}(E_1, E_2, ..., E_n)$

where each E_i is an expression. Its value is the *n*-tuple with components the values of $E_1, E_2, ..., E_n$, in that order.

The only operators for tuples are *equality* and *inequality*:

$Tu_1 = Tu_2 \quad Tu_1 \neq Tu_2$

where Tu_1 and Tu_2 are tuples of the same type. $Tu_1 = Tu_2$ is **true** if each component of Tu_1 is equal to the corresponding component of Tu_2, **false** otherwise. $Tu_1 \neq Tu_2$ is **true** if $Tu_1 = Tu_2$ is **false** and vice versa. Tu_1 and Tu_2 must be flat.

5.6.3 Examples

Product types are used in function and operation signatures to allow more than one parameter and result:

polar : $\mathbb{R} \times \mathbb{R} \rightarrow \mathbb{R} \times \mathbb{R}$

takes two Cartesian coordinates and returns the corresponding polar coordinates.

It is not usually used for a named type, where composite types are generally to be preferred as they enforce strong typing and allow fields to be named.

Values of product types can be handled by tuple patterns (see section 6.2) which allow the individual components of a tuple to be named. Thus the definition of the function *polar* specified above would have to be written implicitly (see section 7.2) using a tuple pattern:

5.6 Compound Types – Product values (tuples)

$polar\ (x, y : \mathbb{R})\ res : \mathbb{R}$
  post let $mk\text{-}(r, \theta) = res$ **in**
    $(r \geq 0)\ \wedge\ (0 \leq \theta)\ \wedge\ (\theta < \pi)\ \wedge\ (x = r \times cos\ (\theta))\ \wedge$
    $(y = r \times sin\ (\theta))$
  -- θ is indeterminate if $x = y = 0$.

Table 17 Tuple operators and expressions

expression	signature & value
$mk\text{-}(E_1, ..., E_n)$	$T_1 \times ... \times T_n \rightarrow (T_1 \times ... \times T_n)$; tuple construction: n-tuple of type $T_1 \times ... \times T_n$ with components E_i
$X_1 = X_2$	$T \times T \rightarrow \mathbb{B}$; equality: X_1 and X_2 have equal components in the same order. X_1 and X_2 must be flat
$X_1 \neq X_2$	$T \times T \rightarrow \mathbb{B}$; inequality: $\neg (X_1 = X_2)$

5.7 Union and optional types

5.7.1 Syntax

union type expression = type expression, '|', type expression;

optional type expression = '[', type expression, ']';

nil literal = 'nil';

5.7.2 Meaning

A *union type expression* has the form:

$T_1 | T_2$

where T_1 and T_2 are type expressions. It denotes the *union type* of the types T_1 and T_2, which contains all the values of type T_1 and all the values of type T_2. T_1 and T_2 may be any types; if they have elements in common then those elements appear once only in the union.

Since a union type expression is a type expression, the syntax allows unions of any finite number of types: $T_1 | T_2 | ... | T_n$. There is no ambiguity here as the union type operator '|' is associative: $(T_1 | T_2) | T_3$ is the same type as $T_1 | (T_2 | T_3)$. The type operator '|' is also commutative: $T_1 | T_2$ is the same as $T_2 | T_1$.

The *optional type* [T] is the type T | Nil , where Nil is used here to denote the predefined *nil type* containing only the *nil value*, denoted by the *nil literal* **nil**. **nil** is conventionally used to stand for the absence of a value There is no way to denote the nil type itself in VDM-SL; it can be introduced only by an optional type expression. There is no type membership expression for the nil type; equality must be used: E = **nil**.

The optional type brackets distribute over type union: $[T_1 | T_2]$ is the same as $[T_1] | T_2$ and as $T_1 | [T_2]$; but not over other type constructors. For example, the following are all distinct types:

$\mathbb{N} \xrightarrow{m} \mathbb{N}$ $[\mathbb{N}] \xrightarrow{m} \mathbb{N}$ $\mathbb{N} \xrightarrow{m} [\mathbb{N}]$ $[\mathbb{N}] \xrightarrow{m} \mathbb{N}$

$[\mathbb{N}] \xrightarrow{m} [\mathbb{N}]$ $[[\mathbb{N}]] \xrightarrow{m} \mathbb{N}]$ $[\mathbb{N}] \xrightarrow{m} [\mathbb{N}]$ $[[\mathbb{N}] \xrightarrow{m} [\mathbb{N}]]$

5.7 Compound Types – Union and optional types

5.7.3 Examples

In general, union types should be used sparingly, as they effectively break strong typing and allow type errors to occur. It is usually better to declare two functions on different types than one function on their union. The main use of union types is with quote types, to create what are effectively enumeration types:

Colour = RED | GREEN | BLUE

Another use is to add one or more special values to the result of a function or operation to indicate exceptional conditions:

quadratic: $\mathbb{R} \times \mathbb{R} \times \mathbb{R} \rightarrow$ (*Roots* | COMPLEX-ROOTS)

where:

Roots :: ROOT1 : $\mathbb{R}$
ROOT2 : $\mathbb{R}$

Another example, from Appendix C.1, is:

Drink = *Tea-or-coffee* | CHOCOLATE

where tea and coffee have various options but chocolate is fixed.

Optional types have similar uses to union types, where the exceptional condition is 'nonexistent'. This is often useful in composite types, for example:

Name ::   FORENAME   : char^+
              INITIAL   : [*Letter*]
              SURNAME   : char^+

and in parameter and result types, see for example *RESULT* in Appendix C.2.

As an example of type matching with union types, consider:

let $x : \mathbb{N} \xrightarrow{m} \mathbb{N} \mid \mathbb{N}^+$ **be st** $x(1) = 0$ **in** ...

5.7 Compound Types – Union and optional types

Here x could be a map or a set, and either would be acceptable in the context of the expression $x(1) = 0$. However if the whole expression is:

let $x : \mathbb{N} \xrightarrow{m} \mathbb{N} \mid \mathbb{N}^+$ **be st** $x(1) = 0$ **in tl** $x \mathbin{\widetilde{}} [0]$

the x must be a sequence and the ambiguity is resolved. It would be invalid to write:

let $x : \mathbb{N} \xrightarrow{m} \mathbb{N} \mid \mathbb{N}^+$ **be st** $x(1) = 0$ **in tl** $x \mathbin{\widetilde{}} [(x \circ x)(2)]$

which places contradictory requirements on the type of x; but it is valid to write:

types
    $Map = \mathbb{N} \xrightarrow{m} \mathbb{N}$
    $Seq = \mathbb{N}^+$
    ...
let $x : Map \mid Seq$ **be st** $x(1) = 0$ **in**
    if $is\text{-}Seq(x)$ **then tl** x **else** $(x \circ x)(2)$

5.8 Compound Types – Function values

5.8 Function values

5.8.1 Syntax

    function type expression = discretionary type expression, '→', type expression;

    discretionary type expression = type expression | '(', ')';

    function application = expression, '(', [expression list], ')';

    function infix operator = '↑' | '∘';

    general infix operator = '=' | '≠';

    lambda expression = 'λ', type bind list, '·', expression;

5.8.2 Meaning

A *function type expression* has one of the forms:

$$T_1 \rightarrow T_2 \qquad () \rightarrow T_2$$

where T_1 and T_2 are type expressions. It denotes the *function type* which contains all functions which take a parameter of type T_1 (first form) or no parameter (second form) and return a value of type T_2. Function values may be created by lambda expressions (see below), or by function definitions, which are described in chapter 7.

A function of two or more parameters is considered as a function of a single parameter of a product type.

Type definitions may not be recursive *through* function types, though they may be recursive *over* them. That is, no chain of definitions derived from a set of recursive type definitions from a type back to itself may pass through a function type expression. For example, the following is valid:

$$T = T \times T \mid \mathbb{N} \rightarrow \mathbb{N}$$

but the following is not:

$$T = \mathbb{N} \times \mathbb{N} \mid T \rightarrow T$$

Function types and types derived from them and values of those types are called *nonflat types* and *nonflat values*; they are almost "first-class

5.8 Compound Types – Function values

citizens" in VDM-SL; that is, they can be used in most circumstances in which other types and values can be used. Exceptions are as follows:

- Nonflat types may not be parameter or result types of operations; see section 8.1. They can however be parameter and result types of functions (except the result types of implicitly defined functions), see chapter 7.

- Set values may not contain nonflat values, and set type constructors may not be applied to nonflat types; see section 5.2.

- Map values may not contain nonflat values in the domain, and map type constructors may not be applied to nonflat types as domain types; see section 5.3.

- State variables and local variables from declaration preambles must have flat types; see section 3.4 and 9.2.

- Equality and inequality are not defined for nonflat values; see section 6.3.

A *function application* has the form:

$F(E_1, ..., E_n)$

where F is a function of n arguments ($n \geq 0$) and $E_1, ..., E_n$ are expressions (the *actual parameters*). The expressions E_i must belong to the corresponding parameter types of the function F, and must satisfy any precondition of F. Its value is the result of applying function F to the values of the E_i as follows. Each formal parameter pattern Pt_i from the function heading of F is matched to the corresponding argument value E_i. The bindings from these matchings are then used to evaluate the function result. The patterns are all matched at once; any repeated pattern identifiers must match the same value at each occurrence. If any match fails, the application is undefined. If the precondition of the function F is **false**, then the value returned by F may or may not be defined.

There are two function operators and one function constructor. A *function composition* has the form:

$F_1 \circ F_2$

where F_1 and F_2 are function expressions. F_1, but not F_2, may be curried (see section 7.4). It yields the function equivalent to applying first F_2,

5.8 Compound Types – Function values

and then applying F_1 to the result. Thus $F_1 \circ F_2(E_1, ..., E_2)$ is the same as $F_1(F_2(E_1, ..., E_2))$. The result type of F_2 must be contained in the parameter type of F_1 (as a product type, if F_1 has more than one parameter).

A *function iteration* has the form:

$$F \uparrow N$$

where N is a non-negative integer; this is the function equivalent to applying F N times. $F \uparrow 0$ is the identity function which just returns the value of its parameter, and $F \uparrow (N+1) = F \circ (F \uparrow N)$. If $N > 1$, the result type of F must be contained in its parameter type.

The only function constructor is the *lambda expression* with the form:

$$\lambda\, Pt_1 : T_1,\, Pt_2 : T_2,\, ...,\, Pt_n : T_n \cdot E$$

where the Pt_i are patterns, the T_i are type expressions, and E is an expression. The scope of any pattern identifiers in the patterns Pt_i is the expression E. This is an explicit expression for a function, equivalent to the function F defined by the explicit function definition:

$$F : T_1 \times T_2 \times ... \times T_n \rightarrow T$$
$$F\,(Pt_1, Pt_2, ..., Pt_n) \triangleq E$$

where T is the type of the expression E. As a function defined by a lambda expression has no name, no precondition and postcondition functions are implicitly declared. A function defined by a lambda expression can be curried by nesting another abstraction within it as the expression E:

$$\lambda\, Pt_1 : T_1,\, ...,\, Pt_n : T_n \cdot \lambda\, Pt_1' : T_1',\, ...,\, Pt_m' : T_m' \cdot ... \cdot E$$

A lambda expression can define a recursive function. A lambda expression cannot be polymorphic.

5.8.3 Examples

Many examples of functions are given in chapter 7. VDM-SL allows functions to be incorporated into compound values, so that sequences of functions, maps to functions, and so on (but not sets of functions or maps from functions) are all possible. These do not occur every day, but can be very useful on occasion. For example, the function keys of a pocket

5.8 Compound Types – Function values

calculator could be represented as a map from quote values representing the keys to functions performing the required function:

types
$\quad$ Key = ADD | SUBTRACT | MULTIPLY | DIVIDE
values
$\quad$ Fn-map : Key $\xrightarrow{m}$ ($\mathbb{Q} \times \mathbb{Q} \rightarrow \mathbb{Q}$) $\triangleq$
$\quad\quad$ {ADD $\mapsto$ $\lambda x : \mathbb{Q}, y : \mathbb{Q} \cdot x + y, ...$ }

A single operation could then be used to represent pressing any of the keys.

Lambda expressions are useful in conjunction with let statements and expressions to introduce local function definitions:

let $f = \lambda x : \mathbb{R} \cdot a \times x \times x + b \times x + c$ **in** ...

As an example of function composition, if $sin : \mathbb{R} \rightarrow \mathbb{R}$ and $log : \mathbb{R} \rightarrow \mathbb{R}$ have their usual mathematical meanings, then $log \circ sin$ is the log sin function (the value 0 could be excluded by a precondition on *log*).

Table 18   Function operators and expressions

operator	function type and value
$F(E_1, ..., E_n)$	$(T_1 \rightarrow T_2) \times T_1 \rightarrow T_2$: function application; the result of applying F to the parameter tuple $mk\text{-}(E_1, ..., E_n)$
$F_1 \circ F_2$	$(T_2 \rightarrow T_3) \times (T_1 \rightarrow T_2) \rightarrow (T_1 \rightarrow T_3)$: function composition; the function $\lambda x \cdot F_1(F_2(x))$
$F \uparrow N$	$(T \rightarrow T) \times \mathbb{N} \rightarrow (T \rightarrow T)$: function iteration; F composed with itself N times
$\lambda\ Pt_1:T_1, ..., Pt_n:T_n \cdot E$	$T_1 \times ... \times T_n \times T \rightarrow (T_1 \times ... \times T_n \rightarrow T)$: lambda expression: the function F of type $T_1 \times ... \times T_n \rightarrow T$, where T is the type of E, defined by $F(Pt_1, ..., Pt_n) \triangleq E$

6 Expressions

6.1 General

6.1.1 Syntax

    expression = unary expression | binary expression
      | complex expression | composite expression | quantified expression
      | iota expression | bracketed expression | application
      | function instantiation | field selection | lambda expression
      | type membership expression | undefined expression
      | symbolic literal | name | set expression | sequence expression
      | map expression | record expression | tuple expression;

    bracketed expression = '(', expression, ')';

    application = map application | sequence application
      | function application;

    undefined expression = **'undefined'**;

    expression list = expression, {',', expression};

6.1.2 Meaning

Expressions allow values to be combined in fixed ways to form other values. They are divided syntactically into the following classes.

- *Unary* and *binary expressions*. These are the familiar operator/operand expressions of mathematics and imperative programming languages. The operators include arithmetic, logical, and set-theoretic operators, and special operators for maps and sequences. See section 6.3 for a general description, and individual sections of chapters 4 and 5 for operators applicable to particular types. The equality and inequality operators = and ≠ are defined for all flat types: if E_1 and E_2 are any flat values, then $E_1 = E_2$ has the value **true** or **false** (of type $\mathbb{B}$) according as E_1 and E_2 denote the same value or not; $E_1 \neq E_2$ has the value **false** or **true** correspondingly.

6.1 Expressions – General

- *Complex expressions*. These allow the introduction of variables local to an expression. See section 6.4.

- *Composite expressions*. These express the selection of one out of two or more expressions according to the value of some variable or expression. See section 6.5.

- *Quantified expressions*. These are logical expressions using quantifiers, taking logical values **true** or **false** according to the existence of elements in some sets and/or types satisfying some Boolean expressions. See section 6.6.

- *Iota expression*. This is similar in form to a quantified expression; the value is the unique element of a set or type satisfying a Boolean expression. See section 6.6.

- *Bracketed expression*. This is just a syntactic convenience for grouping subexpressions for readability or to change the operator precedence. The bracketed expression:

    (E)

    has the same value as the expression E.

- *Applications*. These express the application of a rule to a value (or, for a function, to 0 or more values) to yield another value; the rule can be a function, a map, or a sequence (yielding the element corresponding to an index).

- *Function instantiation*. This applies a polymorphic function to a sequence of types to yield a true function; see section 7.5.

- *Field selection*. This applies a field name to a record, yielding the value of the field denoted by the field name. See section 5.5.

- *Lambda expression*. This allows a function to be defined by giving the result of applying the function to an arbitrary set of arguments. See section 5.8.

- *Type membership expression*. This allows a value to be tested for membership of a basic or compound type, for example to distinguish the components of a union type. See section 3.2.

6.1 Expressions – General

- The *undefined expression* is **undefined**. It is used in an explicit function definition to indicate that there is no defined value. See section 7.3.

- *Symbolic literals* and *names*. These are the basic operands from which expressions are built up. See section 2.3 for literals and section 10.4 for names.

- *Set*, *map*, *sequence*, *record*, and *tuple expressions*. These are particular forms of expression allowing values of those compound types to be modified or built up from values of the base types. They are described with the corresponding composite types. See sections 5.2, 5.3, 5.4, 5.5, and 5.6 respectively.

6.2 Patterns and binds

6.2.1 Syntax

pattern = pattern identifier | dont care | match value | set pattern
 | sequence pattern | tuple pattern | record pattern;

pattern identifier = identifier;

dont care = '-';

match value = '(', expression, ')';

set pattern = set enumeration pattern | set union pattern;

set enumeration pattern = '{', pattern list, '}';

set union pattern = pattern, 'υ', pattern;

sequence pattern = sequence enumeration pattern
 | sequence concatenation pattern;

sequence enumeration pattern = '[', pattern list, ']';

sequence concatenation pattern = pattern, '⁀', pattern;

tuple pattern = 'mk-', '(', pattern list, ')';

record pattern = name, '(', pattern list, ')';

pattern list = pattern, {',', pattern};

bind = set bind | type bind;

set bind = pattern, 'ε', expression;

type bind = pattern, ':', type expression;

bind list = bind list item, {',', bind list item};

bind list item = pattern list, 'ε', expression
 | pattern list, ':', type expression;

type bind list = type bind, {',', type bind};

pattern or bind = pattern | bind;

6.2.2 Meaning

A *pattern* is a template for a value of a particular class of type, with part or all of the value undefined. A *pattern identifier*, a *dont care*, and a *match value* can be used for any type, and represents the whole value. The other forms of pattern are used for particular kinds of compound

6.2 Expressions – Patterns and binds

type. An occurrence of a pattern serves to declare the pattern identifiers it contains; the scope of these declarations is called the *scope* of the pattern.

A pattern is used in various ways in different contexts. In some cases it is used to represent every value of a type (as in an invariant) or of a set (as in a set bind in a quantified expression). In other cases a pattern is used to refer to a particular value of a type or, more usually, to some or all of its components (as in a let expression). In all cases the use of a pattern involves *matching* the pattern to a value; that is, checking whether the value fits the template defined by the pattern. If the matching succeeds, the pattern is said to *match* the value; any pattern identifiers in the pattern are then *bound* to their matched component values, that is, they are declared as new names for those values in the appropriate scope. Each such association of a value with a pattern identifier is called a *binding* of the identifier to the value. In most cases the pattern must match some value or values, but in some cases (as in a cases expression or statement) it need not. These bindings hold throughout the scope of the pattern.

Patterns may contain repeated pattern identifiers; in order for the pattern to match a value, each occurrence of a pattern identifier must be matched to the same value. In some cases, for example a function application, several patterns are matched to values at the same time; the effect is as though the patterns and values were combined into a single tuple pattern and tuple enumeration respectively, and the tuple pattern were matched to the tuple enumeration value. That is, a pattern identifier occurring in more than one pattern must be matched to the same value at each occurrence; and any identifiers in match values in the patterns have there meanings defined outside the whole set of patterns.

Matching is defined recursively as follows.

- A *pattern identifier* matches any value, of any type. The identifier is bound to the value.

- A *dont care* matches any value, of any type. No binding occurs.

- A *match value* (E) matches only the value of the expression E; no binding occurs. If the match value occurs within a larger pattern Pt, E is evaluated before Pt is matched, so if E contains any pattern identifiers from Pt they retain their previous meanings.

6.2 Expressions – Patterns and binds

- A *set enumeration pattern* $\{Pt_1, Pt_2, ..., Pt_n\}$ matches any set value S for which each pattern Pt_i matches a distinct element of S; all elements of S must be matched.

- A *set union pattern* $Pt_1 \cup Pt_2$ matches any set value S for which Pt_1 matches a subset S_1 of S and Pt_2 matches the set $S - S_1$ containing the other elements of S (those not matched to Pt_1).

- A *sequence enumeration pattern* $[Pt_1, Pt_2, ..., Pt_m]$ matches any sequence value Q for which each pattern Pt_i matches the corresponding sequence element $Q(i)$; **len** Q must be m.

- A *sequence concatenation pattern* $Pt_1 \frown Pt_2$ matches any sequence value Q which is the concatenation of subsequences $Q_1 \frown Q_2$ where Pt_1 matches Q_1 and Pt_2 matches Q_2.

- A *record pattern* $mk\text{-}Id(Pt_1, Pt_2, ..., Pt_n)$ matches any record value R of type with tag Id for which the patterns Pt_i match the fields of R in order. All the fields of the record value must be matched.

- A *tuple pattern* $mk\text{-}(Pt_1, Pt_2, ..., Pt_n)$ matches any n-tuple (value of a product type with n components) for which each Pt_i matches the corresponding component of the tuple value, in order.

Matching can be looked at as follows: a pattern Pt matches a value v if values can be substituted for the pattern variables of Pt so that Pt = v is **true**. Those values are then bound to the pattern identifiers of Pt. The only complication is that in a set enumeration pattern $\{Pt_1, Pt_2, ..., Pt_n\}$ the values of the Pt_i must all be different, and in a set union pattern $Pt_1 \cup Pt_2$, Pt_1 and Pt_2 must be disjoint (here $\cup$ represents *disjoint union*).

A *bind* is used to associate a pattern with a type or a set, either to define the values which the pattern is representing, or to limit the choice of values for the pattern to represent. In the former case, a bind implies a collection of combinations of bindings for the pattern identifiers of the binds. For example the tuple type bind $mk\text{-}(x, y) : \mathbb{R} \times \mathbb{B}$ implies all combinations of bindings of x to a real number and y to a truth value.

A *set bind* has the form:

6.2 Expressions – Patterns and binds

$Pt \in S$

where Pt is a pattern and S is a set expression; the associated values are those of the elements of the set S.

A *type bind* has the form:

$Pt : T$

where Pt is a pattern and T is a type expression; the associated values are all those of the type T.

In a bind list, each bind list item $Pt_1, Pt_2, ... \in S$ or $Pt_1, Pt_2, ... : S$ is equivalent to the sequence of binds $Pt_1 \in S$, $Pt_2 \in S$, ... or $Pt_1 : T$, $Pt_2: T$, ... All the patterns in a bind list are matched simultaneously.

Patterns are summarized in Table 19. The type expression on the right of each "signature" indicates the type constraints on values that the pattern matches.

6.2.3 Examples

Patterns are used in the following contexts; see the appropriate sections for examples.

- Invariant and initialization definitions: sections 3.2, 3.4.
- Set, map, and sequence comprehensions: sections 5.2, 5.3, 5.4.
- Complex expressions: section 6.4.
- Cases expressions: section 6.5.
- Quantified, iota, and lambda expressions: sections 6.6, 5.8.
- Function and operation definitions: sections 7.2, 7.3, 8.2, 8.3.
- Bind preambles: section 9.2.
- Handlers: section 9.3.
- Sequence and set loops: section 9.6.
- Cases commands: section 9.7.

6.2 Expressions – Patterns and binds

Table 19 Patterns

pattern	matching value
Id	$() \rightarrow T$; pattern identifier: matches any value (bound to Id)
-	$() \rightarrow T$; dont care: matches any value (no binding)
(E)	$T \rightarrow T$; match value: matches the value of E (no binding)
{Pt$_1$, ..., Pt$_n$}	$T \times ... \times T \rightarrow T$-**set**; set enumeration pattern: matches a set of n elements, matched to the Pt$_i$ in some order
Pt$_1$ ∪ Pt$_2$	T-**set** $\times$ T-**set** $\rightarrow$ T-**set**; set union pattern: matches a set $S_1 \cup S_2$ where Pt$_1$ matches S_1, Pt$_2$ matches S_2, and $S_1 \cap S_2 = \{\}$
[Pt$_1$, ..., Pt$_m$]	$T \times ... \times T \rightarrow T^*$; sequence enumeration pattern: matches a sequence Q of m elements, each Pt$_i$ matching Q(i)
Pt$_1$ ⁀ Pt$_2$	$T^* \times T^* \rightarrow T^*$; sequence concatenation pattern: matches a sequence Q_1 ⁀ Q_2 where Pt$_i$ matches Q_i
mk-Id(Pt$_1$, ..., Pt$_n$)	$T_1 \times ... \times T_n \rightarrow T$; record pattern: a record R of type T = **compose** Id **of** T_1, ...,T_n **end**, where the Pt$_i$ match the fields of R in order
mk-(Pt$_1$, ..., Pt$_n$)	$T_1 \times ... \times T_n \rightarrow (T_1 \times ... \times T_n)$; tuple pattern: a tuple value for which the Pt$_i$ match the components of the value in order

6.3 Unary and binary expressions

6.3.1 Syntax

   unary expression = prefix expression | postfix expression;

   prefix expression = prefix operator, expression;

   postfix expression = expression, postfix operator;

   prefix operator = logical prefix operator | arithmetic prefix operator
     | set prefix operator | sequence prefix operator
     | map prefix operator;

   postfix operator = map postfix operator;

   binary expression = expression, infix operator, expression;

   infix operator = general infix operator | logical infix operator
     | arithmetic infix operator | set infix operator
     | sequence infix operator | map infix operator
     | function infix operator;

   general infix operator = '=' | '≠';

6.3.2 Meaning

A *unary* or *binary expression* is a combination of operands and operators denoting a value of one of a particular class of types, as shown in Tables 20 and 21. Map inverse (see section 5.3) is the only *postfix* unary operator (placed after the operand); all other unary operators are *prefix* (placed before the operand). All binary operators are *infix* (placed between the two operands).

Operator precedence is a means of reducing the necessity for parentheses in an expression containing different operators: an operator with a greater precedence is evaluated before one with less precedence. For instance, the operator '×' has a greater precedence than '+', so in the expression 2 × 3 + 4 the subexpression 2 × 3 is evaluated first to give 6, then 6 + 4 is evaluated to give 10. Parentheses can be used to emphasise or override the precedences: 2 × 3 + 4 = (2 × 3) + 4 = 10, but 2 × (3 + 4) = 14.

Binary operators have precedences from 2 to 7 inclusive. These are shown in Table 21. The unary operators all have the same precedence of

6.3 Expressions – Unary and binary expressions

8, greater than for any binary operator; so ¬ A ∧ B means (¬ A) ∧ B and not ¬ (A ∧ B).

Applicative expressions (applications, function instantiations, subsequence expressions, sequence modifications, and field selections) have an even higher precedence of 9, so that for example x ⁀ y(1) means x ⁀ (y(1)) and not (x ⁀ y)(1). Each of these expressions is syntactically closed on the right but open on the left: it starts with an expression and finishes with a delimiter. The maximum precedence in effect means that the shortest possible expression is taken as the left operand.

Expressions which are closed on the left and open on the right (complex, if, quantified, iota, and lambda expressions) on the other hand have the lowest precedence of 1. This means that the longest possible expression is taken; so **if** x=0 **then** 0 **else** 1/x means **if** x=0 **then** 0 **else** (1/x), and not (**if** x=0 **then** 0 **else** 1)/x.

Operator association allows omission of parentheses in an expression containing the same operator repeated, or operators with the same precedence. *Left association* means that the operators are evaluated from left to right, *right association* means they are evaluated from right to left. Operators which cannot be repeated (because they give results of different types to their operands) and associative operators (where the order of evaluation makes no difference to the result) need have no association when used alone, but may do so when mixed with other operators of equal precedence. Parentheses can be used to emphasise or override operator association. For instance, + and - have equal precedence and left association, so that 4 - 2 + 1 means (4 - 2) + 1 or 3, not 4 - (2 + 1) or 1. Association of binary operators is shown in Table 21 (L = left association, R = right association, X = no association).

The meanings of the operators are given in the sections defining the types of the operands (see Tables 20 and 21). Note that the *equality* and *inequality* operators = and ≠ apply to operands of all flat types: $E_1 = E_2$ is **true** if E_1 and E_2 have the same value and **false** otherwise. This is explained in more detail for each type of operand in the appropriate section.

6.3.3 Examples

The VDM-SL operator precedences and associations are designed to minimize the necessity for the use of parentheses in expressions while

6.3 Expressions – Unary and binary expressions

avoiding flagrant breaches of convention and too many different precedences. Complicated expressions should be made readable by judicious use of parentheses. Precedences can be emphasised also by spacing, with a larger spacing around operators of less precedence, for example in:

$$A \wedge B \Rightarrow C \vee D$$

Care is needed with some unary operators where convention and the VDM-SL rules are at odds:

$$-3 \uparrow 2$$

has the value 9, not as might be expected −9.

There is also a problem with the relative precedence of relational and Boolean operators; the precedences chosen give the expected meaning to expressions such as:

$$a \wedge b \Leftrightarrow \neg(\neg a \vee \neg b)$$

but not to expressions (common in preconditions and postconditions) such as:

$$a = a^{\leftarrow} \wedge b = b^{\leftarrow} + 1 \wedge c = c^{\leftarrow} + 2$$

which must be explicitly written as:

$$(a = a^{\leftarrow}) \wedge (b = b^{\leftarrow} + 1) \wedge (c = c^{\leftarrow} + 2)$$

A binary operator with no association (X in Table 21) must be enclosed in parentheses if it is preceded or followed by an operator of equal precedence. Thus the following expressions are ill-formed:

$$a < b \Leftrightarrow c < d$$
$$a \Rightarrow b \Rightarrow b \vee \neg a$$
$$\textit{set-1} \triangleleft \textit{map-1} \triangleright \textit{set-2}$$
$$10 \uparrow 10 \uparrow 100$$

6.3 Expressions – Unary and binary expressions

and should be replaced by the following (assuming the apparently intended meanings):

$(a < b) \Leftrightarrow (c < d)$

$(a \Rightarrow b) \Rightarrow b \vee \neg a$

$(\text{set-1} \triangleleft \text{map-1}) \triangleright \text{set-2}$ or $\text{set-1} \triangleleft (\text{map-1} \triangleright \text{set-2})$

$10 \uparrow (10 \uparrow 100)$

Table 20 Unary operators (all with precedence 8) — summary

operator	signature	section
¬	$\mathbb{B} \to \mathbb{B}$	4.2
+	$\mathbb{R} \to \mathbb{R}$	4.3
−	$\mathbb{R} \to \mathbb{R}$	4.3
abs	$\mathbb{R} \to \mathbb{R}$	4.3
floor	$\mathbb{R} \to \mathbb{Z}$	4.3
card	T-set $\to \mathbb{N}$	5.2
$\mathcal{F}$	T-set $\to$ T-set-set	5.2
∩	T-set-set $\to$ T-set	5.2
∪	T-set-set $\to$ T-set	5.2
dom	$(T_1 \xrightarrow{m} T_2) \to T_1$-set	5.3
rng	$(T_1 \xrightarrow{m} T_2) \to T_2$-set	5.3
merge	$(T_1 \xrightarrow{m} T_2)$-set $\to (T_1 \xrightarrow{m} T_2)$	5.3
hd	$T^* \to T$	5.4
tl	$T^* \to T^*$	5.4
len	$T^* \to \mathbb{N}$	5.4
elems	$T^* \to$ T-set	5.4
inds	$T^* \to \mathbb{N}_1$-set	5.4
conc	$T^{**} \to T^*$	5.4
$^{-1}$ (postfix)	$(T_1 \xleftrightarrow{m} T_2) \to (T_2 \xleftrightarrow{m} T_1)$	5.3

6.3 Expressions – Unary and binary expressions

Table 21 Binary operators — summary

operators	association	signature	section
relational operators (precedence 2)			
= ≠	X	$T \times T \to \mathbb{B}$	6.3
⇔	L	$\mathbb{B} \times \mathbb{B} \to \mathbb{B}$	4.2
< ≤ > ≥	X	$\mathbb{R} \times \mathbb{R} \to \mathbb{B}$	4.3
∈ ∉	X	$T \times T\text{-set} \to \mathbb{B}$	5.2
⊆ ⊂	X	$T\text{-set} \times T\text{-set} \to \mathbb{B}$	5.2
implicational operators (precedence 3)			
⇒	L	$\mathbb{B} \times \mathbb{B} \to \mathbb{B}$	4.2
additive operators (precedence 4)			
∨	L	$\mathbb{B} \times \mathbb{B} \to \mathbb{B}$	4.2
+ −	L	$\mathbb{R} \times \mathbb{R} \to \mathbb{R}$	4.3
∪ −	L	$T\text{-set} \times T\text{-set} \to T\text{-set}$	5.2
† ∪	L	$(T_1 \xrightarrow{m} T_2) \times (T_1 \xrightarrow{m} T_2) \to (T_1 \xrightarrow{m} T_2)$	5.3
⁀	L	$T^* \times T^* \to T^*$	5.4
multiplicative operators (precedence 5)			
∧	L	$\mathbb{B} \times \mathbb{B} \to \mathbb{B}$	4.2
× /	L	$\mathbb{R} \times \mathbb{R} \to \mathbb{R}$	4.3
rem mod div	L	$\mathbb{Z} \times \mathbb{Z} \to \mathbb{Z}$	4.3
∩	L	$T\text{-set} \times T\text{-set} \to T\text{-set}$	5.2
∘	R	$(T_2 \to T_3) \times (T_1 \to T_2) \to (T_1 \to T_3)$	5.8
∘	R	$(T_2 \xrightarrow{m} T_3) \times (T_1 \xrightarrow{m} T_2) \to (T_1 \xrightarrow{m} T_3)$	5.3
restrictional operators (precedence 6)			
◁ ◁	X	$T_1\text{-set} \times (T_1 \xrightarrow{m} T_2) \to (T_1 \xrightarrow{m} T_2)$	5.3
▷ ▷	X	$(T_1 \xrightarrow{m} T_2) \times (T_2\text{-set}) \to (T_1 \xrightarrow{m} T_2)$	5.3
exponential operators (precedence 7)			
↑	R	$\mathbb{R} \times \mathbb{R} \to \mathbb{R}$	4.3
↑	R	$(T_1 \to T_2) \times \mathbb{N} \to (T_1 \to T_2)$	5.8
↑	R	$(T_1 \xrightarrow{m} T_2) \times \mathbb{N} \to (T_1 \xrightarrow{m} T_2)$	5.3

6.4 Complex expressions

6.4.1 Syntax

complex expression = definition expression | let expression
| let be expression;

definition expression = **'def'**, pattern or bind, '=', expression,
{',', pattern or bind, '=', expression}, **'in'**, expression;

let expression = **'let'**, pattern or bind, '=', expression,
{',', pattern or bind, '=', expression}, **'in'**, expression;

let be expression = **'let'**, bind, ['be', 'st', expression], **'in'**,
expression;

6.4.2 Meaning

A *complex expression* allows local values to be defined for the scope of a single expression only.

A *definition expression* has the form:

def $Pb_1 = E_1$, $Pb_2 = E_2$, ..., $Pb_n = E_n$ **in** E

where each Pb_i is a pattern Pt_i, a set bind $Pt_i \in S$, or a type bind $Pt_i : T$, each E_i is an expression, and E is an expression. Each pattern Pt_i is matched to the value of E_i in turn, as described in section 6.2, and the bindings from the matching are then used in the evaluation of the rest of the definition expression. The expressions E_i may include state variables and local variables (from declaration preambles, section 9.2); this means that the values to which the pattern identifiers of the Pt_i are bound may vary. A definition expression can be used only in an explicit operation definition. Type and set binds are used to limit the values of the E_i to values of type T or elements of S.

A *let expression* has the form:

let $Pb_1 = E_1$, $Pb_2 = E_2$, ..., $Pb_n = E_n$ **in** E

where the Pb_i, E_i, and E are as for a definition expression. It is similar to a definition expression, but the E_i may not contain variables, and the patterns Pt_i are matched to the values of the expressions E_i at the same

6.4 Expressions – Complex expressions

time. The values to which the pattern identifiers of Pt are bound are therefore constant. Let expressions can be used anywhere, but if used outside an operation definition, E may not contain variables either.

A *let be expression* has one of the following forms:

let Pt ∈ S **be st** B **in** E
let Pt ∈ S **in** E
let Pt : T **be st** B **in** E
let Pt : T **in** E

where Pt is a pattern, B is a Boolean expression, S is a set expression, T is a type expression, and E is an expression (**st** stands for 'such that'). Pt is matched to a value chosen so that when B is evaluated with the bindings from that matching it is **true**; those bindings are then used in the evaluation of E. If the Boolean expression B is not given, it defaults to **true**, which places no constraint on the value to be matched. S or T serves to limit the choice of value to be matched.

6.4.3 Examples

Let expressions are useful for improving readability by contracting complicated expressions used more than once. For example, their use is fairly close to the mathematical convention in expressions such as:

let $d = b \uparrow 2 - 4 \times a \times c$ **in**
   if $d < 0$ **then** undefined **else** $(-b + sqrt(d))/(2 \times a)$

Let be expressions are useful for abstracting away the inessential choice of an element from a set, in particular in formulating recursive definitions over sets:

card : *T*-**set** → ℕ
card(s) =   **if** $s = \{\}$ **then** 0
         else let $e \in s$ **in** *card* $(s - \{e\}) + 1$

Let be expressions are also useful where it is known that an element with some property exists but an explicit expression for such an element is not known or difficult to write:

let *root* **be st** $a \times root \uparrow 3 + b \times root \uparrow 2 + c \times root + d = 0$ **in** ...

6.4 Expressions – Complex expressions

Let and definition expressions provide a convenient way to access the components of a compound value. For a tuple value this is the only way:

    let *mk-(x, y)* = *z* **in** *sqrt(x* ↑ *2 + y* ↑ *2)*

For other compound values there is a choice between using a compound pattern and explicitly extracting the components. For example, with a sequence type, the following expressions are equivalent:

    let *x* ⌢[*y*] = *q* **in** [*y*] ⌢ *x*

    [*q*(**len** *q*)] ⌢ *q*[1 , ... , **len** *q* -1]

Table 22 Complex expressions

expression	value
def $Pb_1=E_1,...,Pb_n=E_n$ **in** E	$(T_1 \times T_1) \times ... \times (T_n \times T_n) \times T \rightarrow T$; definition expression: the value of E in the context of matching each Pt_i to a value of E_i; choice limited to an element of S_i or a value of T_i (Pb_i is $Pt_i : T_i$ or $Pt_i \in S_i$)
let $Pb_1=E_1,...,Pb_n=E_n$ **in** E	$(T_1 \times T_1) \times ... \times (T_n \times T_n) \times T \rightarrow T$; let binding expression: as for definition expression, but no variables allowed in E_i
let Pt $\in$ S **be st** B **in** E **let** Pt : T **be st** B **in** E	$\mathbb{B} \times T \rightarrow T$; let be expression: the value of E in the context of matching Pt to a value that satisfies B; choice limited to an element of S or a value of T.
let Pt $\in$ S **in** E **let** Pt : T **in** E	$T \rightarrow T$; let be expression: the value of E in the context of matching Pt to the value of an element of S or to a value of T. Same as **let** Pt $\in$ S **be st true in** E or **let** Pt : T **be st true in** E

6.5 Composite expressions

6.5.1 Syntax

composite expression = if expression | cases expression;

cases expression = '**cases**', expression, ':',
    expression choice list, [',', others expression choice], '**end**';

expression choice list =
    expression choice, {',', expression choice};

expression choice = pattern list, '→', expression;

others expression choice = '**others**', '→', expression;

if expression =
    '**if**', expression, '**then**', expression,
    {elseif expression clause},
    '**else**', expression;

elseif expression clause = '**elseif**', expression, '**then**',
    expression;

6.5.2 Meaning

Composite expressions allow the choice of one from a number of expressions on the basis of the value of a particular expression.

A *cases expression* has the form:

    cases E: or   **cases** E:
        $Pt_{1,1}, Pt_{1,2}, ... \rightarrow E_1'$, $Pt_{1,1}, Pt_{1,2}, ... \rightarrow E_1'$,
        $Pt_{2,1}, Pt_{2,2}, ... \rightarrow E_2'$, $Pt_{2,1}, Pt_{2,2}, ... \rightarrow E_2'$,
        ...
        $Pt_{n,1}, Pt_{n,2}, ... \rightarrow E_n'$, $Pt_{n,1}, Pt_{n,2}, ... \rightarrow E_n'$,
        others → E'   **end**
    end

where E is an expression, the $Pt_{i,j}$ are patterns (see section 6.2), and the E_i' and E' are expressions. In each expression choice, the scope of any pattern identifiers in the pattern list is the expression E_i' after the →.

This form of expression is a generalization of the familiar form from programming languages. The value is that of the first of the expressions E_i' for which one of the preceding patterns $Pt_{i,j}$ matches the value of the

6.5 Expressions – Composite expressions

expression E; E_i' is evaluated for the bindings from that matching. If no $Pt_{i,j}$ matches E, the value of the cases expression is the value of the expression E′ after **others**. If more than one pattern from a choice matches the expression E, one such matching pattern is chosen.

There is no requirement for any of the patterns to match the value E. The final **others** → E′ need not be provided if the patterns cover all cases.

E must have a defined value, but of the expressions E_i' only the chosen one (for which a pattern $Pt_{i,j}$ matches the value of E) is evaluated. This means that there is no need for the other E_i' to have defined values.

An *if expression* has the form:

>   **if** B_1 **then** E_1
>   **elseif** B_2 **then** E_2
>   ...
>   **elseif** B_n **then** E_n
>   **else** E

where the B_i are Boolean expressions and the E_i and E are expressions of the same type T. This has the value of the first E_i for which B_i is **true**, or of E if none of the B_i is **true**. This is the same as:

>   **cases true**:
> (B_1) → E_1,
> (B_2) → E_2,
>   ...
> (B_n) → E_n,
>   **others** → E
>   **end**

where each expression choice contains a single match value.

The final **else** E must be provided, even if the B_i cover all cases.

The only expressions evaluated are the B_i up to and including the first B_j with the value **true**, and its corresponding E_j.

6.5.3 Examples

The use of if and cases expressions is fairly obvious. The choice between the use of elseif clauses and nested if expressions can be used to indicate

6.5 Expressions – Composite expressions

whether the conditions are seen as being on the same level or in some way at a lower or inner level:

```
if x mod 3 = 0 then ...
elseif x mod 3 = 1 then ...
else         -- x mod 3 = 2 (see below)
...

if prime(n) then ...
else if squarefree (n) then ...
    else ...
```

The else clause is compulsory, but it sometimes helps readability to spell out the final condition as a comment, as in the first example above.

The cases expression:

```
cases str:
    str1 ⁀ ['X'] ⁀ str2 → tl str,
    others → str
end
```

which removes the head from any string *str* containing an X, is valid, although **tl** *str* is not defined if *str* is empty.

The equivalent if expression is:

if ∃ *i* ∈ **inds** *str* · *str*[*i*] = 'X' **then tl** *str* **else** *str*

If *str* is empty, the existential quantification over its index set is always **false**.

6.5 Expressions – Composite expressions

Table 23 Composite expressions

expression	value
if B_1 **then** E_1 **elseif** B_2 **then** E_2 ... **elseif** B_n **then** E_n **else** E	$(\mathbb{B} \times T) \times ... \times (\mathbb{B} \times T) \times T \rightarrow T$; if expression: the value of the first E_i for which B_i is **true**, or if none the value of E
cases E: $Pt_1 \rightarrow E_1,$ ..., $Pt_n \rightarrow E_n,$ **others** $\rightarrow$ E´ **end**	$T_1 \times (T_1 \times T_2) \times ... \times (T_1 \times T_2) \times T_2 \rightarrow T_2$; cases expression: the value of the first E_i for which Pt_i matches E, or if it matches none of them and **others** E´ is present, the value of E´. **others** E´ is optional; if absent, some Pt_i must match E_i

6.6 Quantified and iota expressions

6.6.1 Syntax

quantified expression = universal quantified expression
  | existential quantified expression | unique quantified expression;

universal quantified expression = '∀', bind list, '·', expression;

existential quantified expression = '∃', bind list, '·', expression;

unique quantified expression = '∃!', bind, '·', expression;

iota expression = 'ι', bind, '·', expression;

6.6.2 Meaning

There are three forms of *quantified expression* – universal with ∀, existential with ∃, and unique with ∃! Each yields a Boolean value **true** or **false**, as follows.

A *universal quantified expression* has the form:

∀ Bd_1, Bd_2, ..., Bd_n · B

where each Bd_i is either a set bind $Pt_i \in S_i$ or a type bind $Pt_i : T_i$ (see section 6.2), and B is a Boolean expression. It has the value **true** if matching the patterns Pt_i to every combination of values from S_i or T_i gives bindings for which B is **true**; the value **false** if there is at least one combination of bindings for which B is **false**; and is undefined otherwise. It must be possible to match each pattern Pt_i to all values of S_i or T_i.

An *existential quantified expression* has the form:

∃ Bd_1, Bd_2, ..., Bd_n · B

where the Bd_i and B are as for a universal quantified expression. It has the value **true** if matching the patterns Pt_i to at least one combination of values from S_i or T_i gives bindings for which B is **true**; the value **false** if B is **false** for every combination of bindings; and is undefined otherwise. It is equivalent to ¬∀ Bd_1, Bd_2, ..., Bd_n · ¬ B. It must be possible to match each pattern Pt_i to all values of S_i or T_i.

6.6 Expressions – Quantified and iota expressions

In a universal or existential quantification B need not be defined for every matching, so for example the following is **true** although 0+1/0=2 is undefined:

∃ n : N · n + 1/n = 2

In a universal or existential quantified expression, the binds are applied one at a time rather than all at once, so that bindings from an earlier bind can be used in a later one. A more compact form of bind list is available when a set or type is repeated; see section 6.2.

A *unique quantified expression* has the form:

∃! Bd · B

where Bd is either a set bind Pt ∈ S or a type bind Pt : T and B is a Boolean expression. It has the value **true** if there is one and only one binding of Pt to a value from S or T for which B is **true**; and the value **false** otherwise. It must be possible to match Pt to all values of S or T and B must be defined for each such matching.

An *iota expression* has the form:

ι Bd · B

where Bd is either a set bind Pt ∈ S or a type bind Pt : T and B is a Boolean expression. It yields the value of the element of the set S or the value of the type T which, when Pt is matched to it, gives bindings for which B is **true**. There must be only one such value and only one such set of bindings: ∃! Bd · B must be **true**.

6.6.3 Examples

The commonest uses of quantified expressions are with simple pattern identifiers:

∀ d : Drink · d ∈ **dom** PRICES

which expresses the fact that the map PRICES, of type Drink $\xrightarrow{m}$ Money, is total over the type Drink.

6.6 Expressions – Quantified and iota expressions

In these simple cases universal and existential quantification are like distributed conjunction and distributed disjunction:

$\forall\ x \in \{a, b, c\} \cdot f(x)$ and $\exists\ x \in \{a, b, c\} \cdot f(x)$

are respectively the same as:

$f(a) \wedge f(b) \wedge f(c)$ and $f(a) \vee f(b) \vee f(c)$

In these simple cases also a unique quantified expression can be expressed in terms of universal and existential quantified expressions:

$\exists!\ x \in \{a, b, c\} \cdot f(x)$

is the same as:

$\exists\ x \in \{a, b, c\} \cdot f(x) \wedge \forall\ y \in \{a, b, c\} \cdot f(y) \Rightarrow (y = x)$

This does *not* hold in more general cases; see below.

Quantified expressions with more general patterns are useful for handling compound types, though as usual there is often a choice to be made between a compound pattern and explicit references to the components of a value (see section 6.2). For example, with the type *Tea-or-coffee* (Appendix C.1), a constraint that sweet white drinks were disallowed could be expressed using a record pattern or field selections:

$\forall\ mk\text{-}Tea\text{-}or\text{-}coffee\ (-, w, s)\colon Tea\text{-}or\text{-}coffee \cdot \neg(w \wedge s)$
$\forall\ d\colon Tea\text{-}or\text{-}coffee \cdot \neg(d.\text{WHITE} \wedge d.\text{SWEET})$

Changing the order of quantifiers can change the meaning of a quantified expression if it contains both universal and existential quantifiers:

$\forall\ x\colon \mathbb{Z} \cdot \exists\ y\colon \mathbb{N} \cdot y = x \uparrow 2$

is **true** (every integer has a square) but:

$\exists\ y\colon \mathbb{N} \cdot \forall\ x\colon \mathbb{Z} \cdot y = x \uparrow 2$

is **false** (not every integer has the *same* square).

6.6 Expressions – Quantified and iota expressions

In all cases $\forall\ Bd_1, Bd_2, ..., Bd_n \cdot B = \neg\ \exists\ Bd_1, Bd_2, ..., Bd_n \cdot \neg\ B$ and $\exists\ Bd_1, Bd_2, ..., Bd_n \cdot B = \neg\ \forall\ Bd_1, Bd_2, ..., Bd_n \cdot \neg\ B$.

Only one bind is allowed with $\exists!$ because (unlike $\forall$ and $\exists$) the order of binds is significant:

$$\exists!\ x : \mathbb{Z} \cdot \exists!\ y : \mathbb{Z} \cdot y \uparrow 2 = x$$

is **true** (0 is the only integer with a unique square root); but:

$$\exists!\ y : \mathbb{Z} \cdot \exists!\ x : \mathbb{Z} \cdot y \uparrow 2 = x$$

is **false** (every integer has a unique square). If there is more than one binding, even to the same value of S or T, then the unique quantification is **false**; as for example:

$$\exists!\ \{m, n\} : \mathbb{N} \times \mathbb{N} \cdot m + n = 1$$

The iota expression:

$$\iota\ n : \mathbb{N} \cdot n \uparrow 2 = 4$$

has the value 2, but:

$$\iota\ n : \mathbb{Z} \cdot n \uparrow 2 = 4$$

is undefined, as it has two possible values, 2 and −2.

These expressions all have the lowest possible precedence of 1 (see section 6.3). This means that the longest possible constituent expression is taken: the expression is continued to the right as far as is syntactically possible. For instance:

$$\forall\ d : \textit{Tea-or-coffee} \cdot d.\text{WHITE} \land d.\text{SWEET}$$

means:

$$\forall\ d : \textit{Tea-or-coffee} \cdot (d.\text{WHITE} \land d.\text{SWEET})$$

6.6 Expressions – Quantified and iota expressions

In a quantified or an iota expression, the scope of any pattern identifiers in the bind list or the bind is the expression B after the ·.

Table 24 Quantified and iota expressions

expression	value
∀ Bd$_1$, ..., Bd$_n$ · B	universal quantified expression: **true** if B holds for every set of matching values from the Bd$_i$, **false** otherwise
∃ Bd$_1$, ..., Bd$_n$ · B	existential quantified expression: **true** if B holds for some set of matching values from the Bd$_i$, **false** otherwise
∃! Bd · B	unique quantified expression: **true** if B holds for exactly one matching value from Bd, **false** otherwise
ι Bd · B	iota expression: the unique value matching the pattern in Bd such that B holds. Needs ∃! Bd · B

7 Functions

7.1 Function definitions

7.1.1 Syntax

function definition block =
   'functions', function definition, {';', function definition};

function definition = implicit function definition
   | explicit function definition;

7.1.2 Meaning

A *function* is a means of defining a rule for deriving a value (the *result*) from zero or more other values (the *parameters*). It differs from a map in that the domain and range of a function are not restricted to be finite. On the other hand, there are restrictions on what can be done with a function value, and more proof obligations to fulfil. A function differs from an operation (see chapter 8) in that it cannot refer to or alter the values of variables; a function (even if loosely specified) always returns the same result for the same values of the parameters.

There is a small set of constructors and operators for function values (see section 5.8). Apart from these, a function is declared by a *function definition*. This can be either *implicit*, which defines the result of the function implicitly by giving a condition which it satisfies, or *explicit*, which gives the result explicitly as an expression. Implicit function definitions are described in section 7.2 and explicit functions in section 7.3.

A function may have no parameters, but it must have a result (since otherwise it would be meaningless, as functions have no side-effects). More than one parameter is shown by the use of a product type (section 5.6); the actual parameters are regarded as forming a tuple. Alternatively, an explicitly defined function can be *curried*; in this case an incomplete set of parameters can be provided and the result is a function of the remaining parameters. Curried functions are described in section 7.4.

7.1 Functions – Function definitions

A *polymorphic* function definition is one in which the parameter and result types are not all completely defined. A polymorphic function definition does not define a function; the actual parameter and result types must be supplied to produce a function value before the function is applied. Polymorphic function definitions are always explicit; they are described in section 7.5.

7.2 Implicit function definitions

7.2.1 Syntax

    implicit function definition = identifier, typed parameter clause,
       typed identifier, (['**pre**', expression], '**post**', expression
       | '**is**', '**not**', '**yet**', '**defined**');

    typed identifier = identifier, ':', type expression;

    typed parameter clause = '(', [typed pattern list], ')';

    typed pattern list = pattern list, ':', type expression,
       {',', pattern list, ':', type expression};

7.2.2 Meaning

An *implicit function definition* has the form:

$$F (Pt_1 : T_1, Pt_2 : T_2, ..., Pt_n : T_n) \; Id_R : T$$
post B´

Here F is the identifier to be associated with the function, T_i are the types of the parameters, T is the type of the result, Pt_i are patterns defining the parameters, and Id_R is an identifier giving a name for the result for use in the postcondition, see below. The patterns Pt_i are matched to the actual parameters in a function application, see section 5.8. The type of the function is:

$$T_1 \times T_2 \times ... \times T_n \rightarrow T$$

or if there are no parameters:

$$( ) \rightarrow T$$

The result of the function is defined by the Boolean expression B´. This defines the *postcondition*, the value of B´, which holds between the actual parameter values and the value of the result.

In the most general form, each parameter $Pt_i : T_i$ may be replaced by a typed pattern list Pt_1, Pt_2, ..., Pt_m : T. This is equivalent to a list of m parameters $Pt_1 : T$, $Pt_2 : T$, ..., $Pt_m : T$.

7.2 Functions – Implicit function definitions

An implicit function definition may also include a *precondition*, as in:

F (Pt_1 : T_1, Pt_2 : T_2, ..., Pt_n : T_n) Id_R : T
pre B
post B´

where B is a Boolean expression which defines a condition which limits values of the parameters for which the function must be defined.

The function identifier F is declared with global scope. The scope of any pattern identifiers in the parameters is the expressions B and B´; that of the result identifier is the postcondition expression B´.

An implicit function definition may be *recursive*, that is postcondition (but not the precondition) may, directly or indirectly, contain an application of the function being defined, or of its precondition or postcondition functions.

An implicit function definition allows a function to be *loosely specified*, that is the result is not completely defined for every set of parameter values. Loosely specified functions are interpreted as *underspecified*; the value returned is not completely defined, but it is the same for every application to the same parameter values. Thus the function:

even ( ) e : $\mathbb{N}_1$
post e **div** 2 = 0

returns an even positive integer; while the expression:

even ( ) = 2

may be either **true** or **false**, the expression:

even ( ) = even ( )

is always **true**.

An implicit function definition

F (Pt_1 : T_1, Pt_2 : T_2, ..., Pt_n : T_n)Id_R : T
pre B
post B´

7.2 Functions – Implicit function definitions

defines two Boolean-valued functions, *pre*-F and *post*-F, representing the precondition and postcondition respectively. The identifiers *pre*-F and *post*-F are implicitly declared with global scope. The effect is as if the functions were defined explicitly (see section 7.3) as follows:

$pre\text{-}F : T_1 \times T_2 \times ... \times T_n \rightarrow \mathbb{B}$
$pre\text{-}F\ (Pt_1, Pt_2, ..., Pt_n) \triangleq B$
$post\text{-}F : T_1 \times T_2, \times ... \times T_n \times T \rightarrow \mathbb{B}$
$post\text{-}F\ (Pt_1, Pt_2, ..., Pt_n, Id_R) \triangleq B'\ \textbf{pre}\ B$

Here B and B´ are the precondition and postcondition of the function F; if there is no precondition then B is **true**. B and B´ may be loosely specified.

Every implicit function definition must be implementable: there must be interpretations of the precondition and postcondition such that for any set of actual parameters of the correct types (including invariants) matching the formal parameter patterns and satisfying the precondition, there is a result of the correct type (including the invariant) which, with those parameters, satisfies the postcondition. For the function with heading:

$F\ (Pt_1 : T_1, Pt_2 : T_2, ..., Pt_n : T_n)\ Id_R : T$

the implementability condition is (for some interpretation of *pre*-F and *post*-F):

$\forall\ Pt_1 : T_1, ..., Pt_n : T_n \cdot$
$\quad (inv\text{-}T_1(Pt_1) \land ... \land inv\text{-}T_n(Pt_n) \land pre\text{-}F(Pt_1, ..., Pt_n)$
$\quad \Rightarrow \exists\ Id_R : T \cdot inv\text{-}T(Id_R) \land post\text{-}F(Pt_1, ..., Pt_n, Id_R))$

For example, for the function *max1* defined below, the condition is:

$\forall\ S : \mathbb{N}_1\text{-}\textbf{set} \cdot$
$\quad \textbf{card}\ S \neq 0 \Rightarrow \exists\ m : \mathbb{N}_1 \cdot (m \in S) \land \forall x \in S \cdot m \geq x$

that is, every non-empty finite set of positive integers has a greatest element, which is obviously true.

7.2 Functions – Implicit function definitions

A function may be given a type and named, but not defined, by an *incomplete implicit function definition* of the form:

$$F (Pt_1 : T_1, Pt_2 : T_2, ..., Pt_n : T_n) \; Id_R : T \textbf{ is not yet defined}$$

This means that the function definition (precondition and postcondition) will be supplied later. The parameters supplied in an application of F must match the patterns; and the function definition, when supplied, must define the values of all such applications.

7.2.3 Examples

Here is a simple function to return the largest of a (non-empty) set of positive integers, defined implicitly.

max1 $(S: \mathbb{N}_1\text{-}\textbf{set})\; m : \mathbb{N}_1$
pre card $S \neq 0$
post $m \in S \wedge \forall x \in S \cdot m \geq x$

The precondition and postcondition functions of *max1* are

pre-max1 $: \mathbb{N}_1\text{-}\textbf{set} \rightarrow \mathbb{B}$
pre-max1 $(S) \triangleq S \neq 0$

post-max1 $\mathbb{N}_1\text{-}\textbf{set} \times \mathbb{N}_1 \rightarrow \mathbb{B}$
post-max1 $(S, m) \triangleq m \in S \wedge \forall x \in S \cdot m \geq x$
  pre card $S \neq 0$

For more examples of functions, see Appendix C.

7.3 Explicit function definitions

7.3.1 Syntax

    explicit function definition = identifier, ':', function type expression,
        identifier, parameter clause list, ('≜', expression,
        ['pre', expression] | 'is', 'not', 'yet', 'defined');

    parameter clause list = parameter clause, {parameter clause};

    parameter clause = '(', [pattern list], ')';

    undefined expression = '**undefined**';

7.3.2 Meaning

A function can be explicitly defined by giving an expression for the result in terms of the parameters. This is done by an *explicit function definition*, which has the form:

$$F : T_1 \times T_2 \times \ldots \times T_n \rightarrow T$$
$$F\ (Pt_1, Pt_2, \ldots, Pt_n)$$
$$\triangleq E$$
pre B

Here F is the identifier to be associated with the function, T_i are the types of the parameters, T is the type of the result, Pt_i are patterns defining the parameters, E is an expression of the result type T, involving the parameter pattern variables, and B is a Boolean expression involving the parameter pattern variables. The patterns Pt_i are matched to the actual parameters in a function application, see section 5.8; the result is the value of E evaluated in the context of the bindings from those matchings.

The Boolean expression B, which is optional, defines a precondition which constrains the domain of F as for an implicit function definition. If no precondition is given, it defaults to **true**, and there is no constraint.

An explicit function definition can be *recursive*, that is it can use the function itself (in a function application) in the expression E (but not in the precondition expression B). Several explicit or implicit function definitions can be *mutually recursive*, so that each uses the others in its body. This mutual recursion may also include value definitions, including definitions of function values via lambda expressions. The set of mutually recursive functions and values must satisfy a continuity condition; see

7.3 Functions – Explicit function definitions

the Standard for details. Usually it will be satisfied if there is a way for the recursion to terminate for each function and value.

The interpretation of applications of loosely specified functions holds for applications in a recursive definition: the same function is used for each recursive application. This means in effect that a choice is made of the interpretations of any loosely specified expressions within the function body before the recursive definition is evaluated; each such set of choices gives rise to a possible value of the function.

The *undefined expression*:

undefined

is allowed only in an explicit function definition. It has the effect of an extra precondition, so that any combination of parameter values which leads to an attempt to evaluate it is invalid.

For an explicitly defined function to be implementable, there must be an interpretation of the result and precondition expressions such that for every set of parameter values for which the precondition is **true**, the result expression defines a value of the result type.

A function may be given a type and named, but not defined, by an *incomplete explicit function definition* of the form:

$F : T_1 \times T_2 \times ... \times T_n \rightarrow T$
$F\ (Pt_1, Pt_2, ..., Pt_n)$ **is not yet defined**

The meaning is the same as for an incomplete implicit function definition with **is not yet defined**, see section 7.2.

7.3.3 Examples

Here is the function example of section 7.2 defined explicitly, first using an iota expression to mimic the implicit definition, and second in a recursive style:

$max2 : \mathbb{N}_1\text{-}\mathbf{set} \rightarrow \mathbb{N}_1$
$max2\ (S) \triangleq$
$\iota m \in S \cdot \forall\ x \in S \cdot m \geq x$
pre $card\ S \neq 0$

7.3 Functions – Explicit function definitions

$max3 : \mathbb{N}_1\text{-set} \rightarrow \mathbb{N}_1$

$max3\ (S) \underline{\triangle} $ **let** $n \in S$ **in**
   if $\forall x \in S \cdot n \geq x$ **then** n
   else $max3\ (S - \{n\})$
pre card $S \neq 0$

The implementability conditions here are: for *max2*, that the iota expression is valid:

$\forall S : \mathbb{N}_1\text{-set} \cdot$
   card $S \neq 0 \Rightarrow \exists! m \in S \cdot \forall x \in S \cdot m \geq x$

and for *max3*, that the recursion terminates for every choice of *n* in the let binding expression at each level of the recursion.

The undefined expression is useful in an explicit function definition when the detection of an undefined case is a by-product of the computation of the function result, so that an explicit precondition would repeat most of the function body. A simple example is the function *depth* computing the maximum depth of nesting of a bracketed expression by scanning the expression, incrementing a count for each '(', decrementing it for each ')', and keeping a running maximum. If the count goes negative, or ends non-zero, the expression is ill-formed. The parameters *count* and *max* are supposed to be set zero on the first call.

depth $: \mathbb{N} \times \mathbb{N} \times \text{char}^* \rightarrow \mathbb{N}$

depth(max, count, exp) $\underline{\triangle}$
   if card $exp = 0$ **then**
     if $count \neq 0$ **then undefined else** max
   else
     cases hd exp :
       ('(') $\rightarrow$ *depth(max, count+1, tl exp)*,
       (')') $\rightarrow$ **if** $count < 1$ **then undefined**
                else *depth(***if** $count > max$ **then** $count$ **else** max,
                        count–1, tl exp),
       others $\rightarrow$ *depth(max, count, tl exp)*
     end

7.4 Curried functions

7.4.1 General

An explicit function definition may be *curried* by providing a function type as the result type, as in:

$$F : T_1 \to (T_2 \to (... \to (T_m \to T)...))$$
$$F\ (Pt_1)\ (Pt_2)\ ...\ (Pt_m) \triangleq E$$

Such a function may be said to have order *m*. The parentheses in the signature can be omitted, as the function arrow $\to$ is right associative:

$$F : T_1 \to T_2 \to ... \to T_m \to T$$

In the most general form each T_i is a product type and the Pt_i and $Pt_i : T_i$ are lists:

$$F : T_{1,1} \times T_{1,2} \times ... \to T_{2,1} \times T_{2,2} \times ... \to\ ...\ \to T_{m,1} \times T_{m,2} \times ... \to T$$
$$F\ (Pt_{1,1}, Pt_{1,2}, ...\ )\ (Pt_{2,1}, Pt_{2,2}, ...\ )\ ...\ (Pt_{m,1}, Pt_{m,2}, ...\ ) \triangleq E$$

A curried function application is formed by following the function name F with one or more expression lists in parentheses, each expression list representing a set of actual parameters corresponding to the formal parameter sets in order:

$$F(E_{1,1}, E_{2,1}, ...\ )\ (E_{2,1}, E_{2,2}, ...\ )\ ...\ (E_{m,1}, E_{m,2}, ...\ )$$

If *m* expression lists are supplied, where *m* is the order of the function, the function is *completely applied*, and the result is an ordinary value of the result type T. If *n* expression lists are supplied, where $1 \leq n < m$, the function is *partially applied*: the result is a function on the remaining sets of parameters, of curried type:

$$T_{n+1,1} \times T_{n+1,2} \times ... \to\ ...\ \to T_{m,1} \times T_{m,2} \times ... \to T$$

The result function is derived from F by the following steps:

- deleting the first *n* sets of formal parameters (corresponding to the supplied actual parameters) from the function heading;

7.4 Functions – Curried functions

- replacing the expression E by:

  let $Pt_{1,1} = E_{1,1}$, $Pt_{1,2} = E_{1,2}$, ... **in**
  let $Pt_{2,1} = E_{2,1}$, $Pt_{2,2} = E_{2,2}$, ... **in**
  ...
  let $Pt_{n,1} = E_{n,1}$, $Pt_{n,2} = E_{n,2}$, ... **in** E

This function can then be applied to the next set or sets of actual parameters, and so on until a value is returned.

A curried function definition may also have **is not yet defined** in place of its body, meaning that the definition will be supplied later. See section 7.2.

7.4.2 Examples

Any function of two or more parameters can be curried. For example:

$F\text{-}1 : \mathbb{R} \times \mathbb{R} \rightarrow \mathbb{R}$

$F\text{-}1(x, y) \triangleq x + y$

which returns the sum of its arguments can be curried:

$F\text{-}2 : \mathbb{R} \rightarrow \mathbb{R} \rightarrow \mathbb{R}$

$F\text{-}2(x)(y) \triangleq x + y$

so that $F\text{-}2(3)$ is the function of one argument that adds 3 to its argument.

A curried function can always be replaced by its partial applications; for example for $F\text{-}2$ above:

$F\text{-}2 : \mathbb{R} \rightarrow \mathbb{R} \rightarrow \mathbb{R}$

$F\text{-}2(x) \triangleq \lambda y \cdot x + y$

$F\text{-}1 : \mathbb{R} \times \mathbb{R} \rightarrow \mathbb{R}$

$F\text{-}1(x, y) \triangleq F\text{-}2(x)(y)$

Curried functions are sometimes preferred on stylistic grounds. Apart from that they are useful when dealing extensively with function values. An example is provided by the theory of compiler generators. A computer program of the usual sort can be modelled approximately as a function from its input to its output:

7.4 Functions – Curried functions

Program = Input → Output

A compiler is a program which takes a source text as input and delivers a program as output:

Compiler = Source → Program
or *Compiler = Source → Input → Output*

while an interpreter takes the source text and input at the same time:

Interpreter = Source × Input → Output

A *partial evaluator* is a program that converts a program with two inputs into a program with one input by applying it to a fixed value of the first input:

P-e = (Input1 × Input2 → Output) × Input1 → (Input1 → Output)

A partial evaluator for an interpreter would have the type:

P-e1 = (Source × Input → Output) × Source → (Source → Output)
or *P-e1 = Interpreter × Source → Program*

Partial evaluation of an interpreter is the same as compiling. It follows that a compiler can be generated by partial evaluation of a partial evaluator with respect to an interpreter:

P-e2 = (Interpreter × Source → Program) × Interpreter → (Interpreter → Program)
or *P-e2 = P-e1 × Interpreter → Compiler*

A compiler generator can therefore be created by partially evaluating a partial evaluator with respect to a partial evaluator:

P-e3 = (P-e1 × Interpreter → Compiler) × P-e1 → (Interpreter → Compiler)
or *P-e3 = P-e2 × P-e1 → Compiler-generator*

7.5 Polymorphic function definitions

7.5.1 Syntax

polymorphic function definition =
　identifier, type variable list, ':', function type expression,
　identifier, parameter clause list, ('≙', expression,
　['pre', expression] | 'is', 'not', 'yet', 'defined');

type variable list = '[', type variable identifier,
　{',', type variable identifier}, ']';

function instantiation = expression, '[', type expression,
　{',', type expression}, ']';

type variable identifier = '@', identifier;

7.5.2 Meaning

A *polymorphic function definition* is an explicit function definition in which the parameter and result types are incompletely defined. It has the same form as a normal explicit function definition, except that one or more of the parameter and result types is given by a *polymorphic type expression*, which is a type expression that is or involves a *type variable*; all these type variables are listed in the type variable list. A type variable is an identifier beginning with the special character @; a polymorphic function definition is the only place where it may be used. Implicit function definitions cannot be polymorphic.

In order to get a function from a polymorphic function definition, the actual types to be used for each polymorphic type in the function heading must be specified. This is done by a *function instantiation*, of the form:

　$F[T_1, T_2, ..., T_m]$

in which there is one type expression T_i for each type variable identifier @Id_i in the function heading. The value is the function with each type variable @Id_i replaced throughout by the corresponding type T_i.

Polymorphic function definitions can be mutually recursive, subject to the same continuity condition as for normal function definitions. A polymorphic function definition may include in its body instantiations of polymorphic functions, including itself.

7.5 Functions – Polymorphic function definitions

A polymorphic function may be given a polymorphic signature and name, but not be defined, by an *incomplete polymorphic function definition* of the form:

$$F\ [@Id_1, @Id_2, ..., @Id_m] : T_1 \times T_2 \times ... \times T_n \to T$$
$$F\ (Pt_1, Pt_2, ..., Pt_n)\ \textbf{is not yet defined}$$

The polymorphic function F may be instantiated in the usual way, but the result is as if the instantiated function were declared with **is not yet defined** in place of its body: see section 7.3.

7.5.3 Examples

The following polymorphic functions support the notion of finite *multisets* or *bags*; these are like sets but can contain the same element more than once. They are modelled as maps from the elements to their multiplicity in the multiset; a nonelement is absent from the map (rather than being mapped to 0).

$empty\text{-}bag\ [@elem] : (\ ) \to (@elem \xrightarrow{m} \mathbb{N})$
-- the empty multiset
$empty\ bag(\ ) \triangleq \{\ \}$

$num\text{-}bag\ [@elem] : @elem \times (@elem \xrightarrow{m} \mathbb{N}_1) \to \mathbb{N}$
-- the cardinality of element e in multiset m
$num\text{-}bag(e,m) \triangleq \textbf{if}\ e \in \textbf{dom}\ m\ \textbf{then}\ m(e)\ \textbf{else}\ 0$

$plus\text{-}bag\ [@elem] : @elem \times (@elem \xrightarrow{m} \mathbb{N}_1) \to (@elem \xrightarrow{m} \mathbb{N}_1)$
-- multiset m plus element e
$plus\text{-}bag(e,m) \triangleq m\ \dagger\ [e \mapsto num\text{-}bag[@elem]\ (e,m) + 1]$

$mems\text{-}bag\ [@elem] : @elem \xrightarrow{m} \mathbb{N}_1 \to @elem\text{-}\textbf{set}$
-- the elements of multiset m as a set
$mems\text{-}bag(m) \triangleq \textbf{dom}\ m$

$merge\text{-}bag\ [@elem] : (@elem \xrightarrow{m} \mathbb{N}_1) \times (@elem \xrightarrow{m} \mathbb{N}_1) \to$
$\quad (@elem \xrightarrow{m} \mathbb{N}_1)$
-- union of multisets m-1 and m-2, i.e. all the elements of each
$merge\text{-}bag(m\text{-}1, m\text{-}2) \triangleq [e \mapsto num\text{-}bag[@elem]\ (e, m\text{-}1) +$
$\quad num\text{-}bag[@elem]\ (e, m\text{-}2)\ |\ e \in \textbf{dom}\ m\text{-}1\ \cup\ \textbf{dom}\ m\text{-}2]$

7.5 Functions – Polymorphic function definitions

$\text{diff-bag}\,[@elem] : (@elem \xrightarrow{m} \mathbb{N}_1) \times (@elem \xrightarrow{m} \mathbb{N}_1) \rightarrow$
   $(@elem \xrightarrow{m} \mathbb{N}_1)$
-- difference of multisets: elements of m-1 less those of m-2.
$\text{diff-bag}(m\text{-}1, m\text{-}2) \triangleq [e \mapsto \text{num-bag}[@elem]\,(e, m\text{-}1) -$
   $\text{num-bag}[@elem]\,(e, m\text{-}2) \mid (e \in \textbf{dom}\ m\text{-}1) \land$
   $(\text{num-bag}[@elem]\,(e, m\text{-}1) > \text{num-bag}[@elem]\,(e, m\text{-}2))]$

Using these functions, the vending machine specification of Appendix C.1 could be rewritten with the type *Cash* as multiset of *Coin* and the type *Stock* as multiset of *Ingredient*:

$\text{Stock} = \text{Ingredient} \xrightarrow{m} \mathbb{N}_1$
$\text{Cash} = \text{Coin} \xrightarrow{m} \mathbb{N}_1$

without the invariants. The type *Prices* could also be redefined as multiset of *Drink*, but that would falsify its intended meaning. The initialization of *STOCKS* and *TAKINGS* are simplified to:

$S = \{\}$
$\land\ T = \{\}$

All expressions with operands of type *Stock* or *Cash* now have to be rewritten using instantiations of the multiset functions. For instance in the postcondition of *INSERT-COIN*:

$TAKINGS = TAKINGS^{\leftarrow} \dagger \{new\text{-}coin \mapsto TAKINGS^{\leftarrow}(new\text{-}coin) + 1\}$

is changed to:

$TAKINGS = \text{plus-bag}[Coin](new\text{-}coin, TAKINGS^{\leftarrow})$

The repeated instantiations can be avoided by defining the instantiated functions as values, either locally:

let $\text{plus-cash}: Coin \times (Coin \xrightarrow{m} \mathbb{N}_1) \rightarrow (Coin \xrightarrow{m} \mathbb{N}_1) =$
   $\text{plus-bag}[Coin]\ \textbf{in}\ ...$

or globally:

129

7.5 Functions – Polymorphic function definitions

values
　　$plus\text{-}cash : Coin \times (Coin \xrightarrow{m} \mathbb{N}_1) \rightarrow (Coin \xrightarrow{m} \mathbb{N}_1) =$
　　$plus\text{-}bag[Coin]$

For another way using parameterized modules see section 10.3.

8 Operations

8.1 Operation definitions

8.1.1 Syntax

operation definition block =
  'operations', operation definition, {';', operation definition};

operation definition = implicit operation definition
  | explicit operation definition;

8.1.2 Meaning

An *operation* models the means by which a specified system interacts with the outside world. Like a function, an operation takes parameters and returns a result, but unlike a function it can read and alter values of the state variables. An operation is defined by an *operation definition*.

Operations are defined in a very similar way to functions, and like functions have their own *operation types*, giving the types of the parameters and results. Resultless operations are possible, since it is quite meaningful for an operation just to update the state. Operations can be called like functions, but only within other operations and in a limited number of constructs. There are no operation constructors or operators. Operation definitions cannot be polymorphic. Operations cannot be curried, and cannot take functions as parameters or return functions as results. There are no operation values; all that can be done with an operation is to call it.

Another difference from functions is the treatment of loosely specified operations: these are nondeterministic, that is, they yield all possible values or (to put it more prosaically) yield an undefined value about which nothing can be assumed (except that it belongs to the result type and satisfies the postcondition), not even that it is the same for different operation calls with the same parameter values. This does not mean that the result of a loosely specified operation is necessarily random; an implementation that always delivers the same result is valid, but it is not the only valid implementation.

8.1 Operations – Operation definitions

Like functions, operations may be defined implicitly or explicitly. An implicit operation definition defines the effect of the operation by a postcondition; an explicit operation definition defines it explicitly by means of statements (see chapter 9).

An operation call may terminate normally or abnormally; in the latter case the statement containing the call is terminated and the result of the operation is passed on out. Implicitly defined operations always terminate normally; explicitly defined operations may terminate normally or abnormally.

8.2 Implicit operation definitions

8.2.1 Syntax

    implicit operation definition = identifier, typed parameter clause,
       [typed identifier], [external variable clause],
       (['pre', expression], 'post', expression, [error definition block]
       | 'is', 'not', 'yet', 'defined');

    external variable clause = 'ext', external variable item,
       {external variable item};

    external variable item = mode, name list, [':', type expression];

    mode = 'rd' | 'wr';

    error definition block = 'errs', error definition, {error definition};

    error definition = identifier, ':', expression, '→', expression;

    old name = identifier, '↶';

8.2.2 Meaning

An *implicit operation definition* in the simplest case has one of the forms:

    Op $(Pt_1:T_1, ..., Pt_n:T_n)$
       post B´

    Op $(Pt_1:T_1, ..., Pt_n:T_n)$ $Id_R:T$
       post B´

Here Op is the identifier to be associated with the operation, T_i are the types of the parameters, T is the type of the result, Pt_i are patterns of the corresponding types T_i defining the parameters, and Id_R is an identifier giving a name for the result for use in a postcondition. If the operation has no result then Id_R : T is omitted. T may be a product type, allowing the effect of several results. B´ is a Boolean expression involving the parameter pattern identifiers, the result identifier, and possibly state variables (see below). The meaning is that the result of the operation and its effect on the state are undefined if B´ is **false**.

The operation identifier Op is declared with global scope. The scope of any pattern identifiers in the parameters is the body of the operation (the precondition, postcondition, and error definition block). The scope of the

8.2 Operations – Implicit operation definitions

result identifier is the postcondition B´ and the error postconditions $B_i´$ of the error definition block.

An implicit operation definition may also have a *precondition* of the form:

    pre B

where B is a Boolean expression involving the parameter pattern identifiers and possibly state variables, but not the result identifier. The precondition limits the values of the parameters and the values of the state variables for which the postcondition must be defined to those for which B is **true**.

The name and type of any state variables mentioned in the precondition or postcondition must be given in the *external variable clause*, following the heading; this has the form:

    ext Md_1 $Nm_{1,1}$, $Nm_{1,2}$, ... : T_1
          Md_2 $Nm_{2,1}$, $Nm_{2,2}$, ... : T_2
          ...
          Md_m $Nm_{m,1}$, $Nm_{m,2}$, ... : T_m

where each Md_i is a *mode*, either **rd** (for "read") or **wr** (for "write/read"), the $Nm_{i,j}$ are state variable names, and the T_i are type expressions. Each type T_i must be the same as in the variable definition for each $Nm_{i,j}$ in the state definition, and is of course redundant. If the value of a variable $Nm_{i,j}$ can be altered by the operation, the mode Md_i must be **wr**, otherwise **rd** should be used.

State variables with mode **wr** can occur in the postcondition in two forms: as normal identifiers, when they denote the values of the state variables after the operation, and as *old names* (hooked) denoting the values before the operation. State variables with mode **rd** can occur in the postcondition only as normal identifiers (they have the same value before and after the operation). State variables in the precondition always occur as normal identifiers, denoting their values *before* the operation.

The *error definition block* extends the definition of the operation to values of the parameters and state variables for which the precondition fails to hold. It has the form:

8.2 Operations – Implicit operation definitions

>   **errs** $Id_1 : B_1 \rightarrow B_1'$
> $Id_2 : B_2 \rightarrow B_2'$
>   ...
> $Id_n : B_n \rightarrow B_n'$

Here $n > 0$, and each Id_i is an identifier denoting an *error condition*; its purpose is purely annotatory. Each B_i is an *error precondition*: a Boolean expression involving the parameter pattern identifiers and state variables in the external variable clause (as for a precondition); and each B_i' is an *error postcondition*: a Boolean expression like B_i but also involving the result identifier and the old names of state variables with mode **wr** (as for a postcondition). The effect is to extend the precondition and postcondition so that if an error precondition holds then the effect of the operation is such that the corresponding error postcondition holds. If more than one of the precondition and error precondition hold, then any of the corresponding postconditions may hold. Thus an operation with the conditions:

>   **pre** B
>   **post** B'
>   **errs** $Id_1 : B_1 \rightarrow B_1'$
>   ...
> $Id_n : B_n \rightarrow B_n'$

is equivalent to the same operation with:

>   **pre** $B \lor B_1 \lor B_2 \lor ... \lor B_n$
>   **post** $(B \land B') \lor (B_1 \land B_1') \lor ... \lor (B_n \land B_n')$

The error definitions in the error definition block declare the error identifiers, with the error list as their scope. The error identifiers are just for annotation; but they must all be different.

An implicit operation definition with the heading:

>   Op $(Pt_1 : T_1, Pt_2 : T_2, ..., Pt_n : T_n)$ $Id_R : T$

implicitly defines two functions, *pre*-Op and *post*-Op, representing the precondition and postcondition respectively. The identifiers *pre*-Op and *post*-Op are implicitly declared with global scope. The effect is as if the functions were defined explicitly as follows:

135

8.2 Operations – Implicit operation definitions

pre-Op : $T_1 \times T_2 \times ... \times T_n \times T_1' \times T_2' \times ... \times T_m' \to \mathbb{B}$
pre-Op (Pt_1, Pt_2, ..., Pt_n, Id_1, Id_2, ..., Id_m) $\triangleq$ B

$post$-Op : $T_1 \times T_2 \times ... \times T_n \times T_1' \times T_2' \times ... \times T_m' \times T_1'' \times T_2'' \times ... \times T_k'' \times T \to \mathbb{B}$
$post$-Op (Pt_1, Pt_2, ..., Pt_n, Id_1, Id_2, ..., Id_m, Id_1', Id_2', ..., Id_k', Id_R) $\triangleq$
B' **pre** B

B and B' are the precondition and postcondition of the operation Op. If there is no precondition then B is taken to be **true**. Id_i are all the state variable identifiers (of types T_i') in the external variable clause, and Id_j' are those (of types T_j'') with mode **wr**, in both cases in the same order.

An *old name* has the form

Id ⃖

where Id is a state variable identifier. It is used only in the postcondition of an implicit operation body, and denotes the value of the state variable Id before the operation invocation. The unhooked form Id is used in the postcondition to denote the value after the operation invocation, and in the precondition to denote the value before (as the value after cannot be used in a preconditition). It is needed only for state variables of mode **wr**, as only those can have different values before and after. An old name can also be written, by convention, in the more customary (but harder to typeset) manner with the hook over the identifier: *identifier̂*.

The implementability condition for an implicit operation definition is that for any set of parameters of the correct types (including invariants) satisfying the precondition, and any set of (old) values of the state variables of the correct types (including type and state invariants), there are a result and set of (new) values of the state variables of the correct type (including invariants) which with those parameters and old state variable values satisfies the postcondition. Only state variables mentioned in the external variable clause need be considered, and only those with mode **wr** need be considered for the postcondition.

Both precondition and postcondition may be loosely specified; this is interpreted nondeterministically: any of the possible interpretations may be applied at any call. However, if all interpretations of the precondition are **true** for a particular set of parameters and old state values, then the effect of the operation is to produce results and new state values for which all interpretations of the postcondition are **true**. Similarly, if

8.2 Operations — Implicit operation definitions

there is an interpretation of the precondition which is **true** for an input set, then the effect of the operation is such that there is an interpretation of the postcondition which is **true**.

An operation may be declared and named, but not defined, by an *incomplete implicit operation definition* in which the precondition, postcondition, and error definition block are replaced by **is not yet defined**. The meaning is that the operation definition will be supplied later. It can be assumed that the operation definition will respect the parameter and result types and the external variable clause.

8.2.3 Examples

Here is an implicit definition of an operation to update an entry in a database (represented as a map from keys to values) with a new value, either overwriting the previous entry with the same key or, if none, adding a new entry. It returns a result to show which action took place.

    ADD-VALUE (*key*: *Key*, *value*: *Value*) *result*: OVERWRITE|ADD
    ext wr *DATABASE* : *Key* $\xleftrightarrow{m}$ *Value*

    post *DATABASE* := *DATABASE*$^{\leftarrow}$ † [*key* $\mapsto$ *value*] ∧

      result = **if** *key* ∈ **dom** *DATABASE*$^{\leftarrow}$ **then** OVERWRITE **else** ADD

As an example of the use of error conditions, consider the operation *GET-DRINK* of Appendix C.1. As specified, if the machine is out of ingredients or cups, or not enough money has been inserted, then the machine can do anything at all. This is unlikely to be desirable behaviour; error postconditions can be used to cover these situations while leaving the specification of the normal case unchanged. In the revised specification below, the result type has been enhanced to allow an error indication to be returned instead of a drink.

    GET-DRINK(*choice* : *Drink*) *goods* : *Drink* | LOW-STOCK | NO-CUPS
      | MORE-MONEY
    ext w r *BALANCE* : *Money*
        w r *CUPS* : $\mathbb{N}$
        w r *STOCKS* : *Stock*
        r d *PRICES* : *Prices*
    pre (∀ *i* ∈ *INGREDIENTS* (*choice*) · *STOCKS*(*I*) > 0)
      ∧ (*CUPS* > 0)
      ∧ (*BALANCE* ≥ *PRICES* (*choice*))

8.2 Operations – Implicit operation definitions

post $(BALANCE = BALANCE^{\leftarrow} - PRICES(choice))$
$\land \ (CUPS = CUPS^{\leftarrow} - 1)$
$\land \ (STOCKS = STOCKS^{\leftarrow} \dagger$
$\quad \{i \mapsto STOCKS^{\leftarrow}(i) - 1 \mid i \in INGREDIENTS(choice)\})$
$\land \ (goods = choice)$

errs
low-on-stock : $\exists \ i \in INGREDIENTS \ (choice) \cdot STOCKS(i) = 0 \rightarrow$
$\quad (BALANCE = BALANCE^{\leftarrow}) \land (CUPS = CUPS^{\leftarrow})$
$\land \ (STOCKS = STOCKS^{\leftarrow}) \land (goods = LOW\text{-}STOCK)$
out-of-cups : $CUPS = 0 \rightarrow$
$\quad (BALANCE = BALANCE^{\leftarrow}) \land (CUPS = CUPS^{\leftarrow})$
$\land \ (STOCKS = STOCKS^{\leftarrow}) \land (goods = NO\text{-}CUPS)$
more-money-needed : $BALANCE < COST(choice) \rightarrow$
$\quad (BALANCE = BALANCE^{\leftarrow}) \land (CUPS = CUPS^{\leftarrow})$
$\land \ (STOCKS = STOCKS^{\leftarrow}) \land (goods = MORE\text{-}MONEY)$

For more examples of operations see Appendix C.1.

8.3 Explicit operation definitions

8.3.1 Syntax

explicit operation definition =
  identifier, ':', operation type expression,
  identifier, parameter clause,
  [external variable clause],
  ('$\triangle$', statement,
  ['pre', expression]
  | 'is', 'not', 'yet', 'defined');

operation type expression = discretionary type expression, '$\xrightarrow{o}$',
  discretionary type expression;

discretionary type expression = type expression | '(', ')';

8.3.2 Meaning

An *explicit operation definition* has the form:

$Op : T_1 \times T_2 \times ... \times T_n \xrightarrow{o} T$
$Op(Pt_1, ... Pt_n)$
  $\triangle$ St

Here Op is the local identifier to be associated with the operation, T_i are the types of the parameters, T is the type of the result, and St is a statement (which may be compound). T may be a product type, allowing the effect of several results. Either or both of $T_1 \times T_2 \times ... \times T_n$ and T may be replaced by "( )" to show that there is no parameter or no result. All the types T_i and T must be flat. The effect of a call to the operation is to execute the statement St as described in chapter 9. The returned value of St is the result of the operation call, and must be of type T; if T is replaced by "( )" then St must have no returned value.

An explicit operation definition may include a precondition:

$Op : T_1 \times T_2 \times ... \times T_n \xrightarrow{o} T$
$Op(Pt_1, ... Pt_n)$
  $\triangle$ St
  pre B

8.3 Operations – Explicit operation definitions

where B is a Boolean expression involving some or all of the parameter pattern identifiers; B may also involve state variables. It constrains the parameter values and state variable values for which the effect of the operation must be defined, as for an implicit operation definition.

The statement St and the precondition may contain the names of state variables. In the precondition, these denote their values prior to the operation. The values of state variables may be updated within the St by assign commands (see section 9.4). The parameter pattern identifiers may be used in the precondition and in St.

The precondition B and the statement St may be loosely specified; this is interpreted as nondeterminism, so that any call of the operation may apply any combination of interpretations. If all interpretations of the precondition are **true** for some set of parameter values and state variable values, then the effect of the statement St must be the same for all interpretations. The implementability condition is that if some interpretation of the postcondition is **true**, then there is an interpretation of St which produces results of the correct types.

The external variable clause defines all the state variables accessed by the operation, and those which may have their values altered, as for an implicit operation definition. Any state variables accessed by operations called from this operation must be included.

An operation may be declared and named, but not defined, by an *incomplete explicit operation definition* in which the precondition and statement are replaced by **is not yet defined**, meaning that the operation definition will be supplied later. It can be assumed that the operation definition will respect the parameter and result types and the external variable clause.

8.3.3 Examples

Here is an explicit definition of the operation *ADD-VALUE* from section 8.2. For more examples see Appendix C.1.

$$ADD\text{-}VALUE : Key \times Value \xrightarrow{o} OVERWRITE \mid ADD$$
$ADD\text{-}VALUE\ (key,\ value)$
   ext wr $DATABASE : Key \xrightarrow{m} Value\ \triangle$
   if $key \in$ **dom** $DATABASE$
   then $(DATABASE\ (key) := value;$ **return** $OVERWRITE)$
   else $(DATABASE := DATABASE \cup [key \mapsto value];$ **return** $ADD)$

8.4 Operation calls

8.4.1 Syntax

operation call = name, '(', [expression list], ')', ['**using**', state designator];

8.4.2 Meaning

An *operation call* has one of the forms:

$Op(E_1, E_2, ..., E_n)$

$Op(E_1, E_2, ..., E_n)$ **using** Sd

where Op is the name of an operation, and the E_i are expressions (the *actual parameters*) of the types in the parameter clause of Op. The state designator Sd is normally used only when calling an operation from a module other than the one it is declared in; see chapter 10. It defines a record of the same type as the notional state type of the module containing the definition of Op, to be used instead of the state; the value of Sd must satisfy any applicable invariant. An operation call invokes the operation Op with the formal parameter patterns Pt_1, Pt_2 ..., Pt_n matched to the actual parameters $E_1, E_2, ..., E_n$. It returns the result of the operation and an indication of whether it terminated normally or abnormally.

An operation call can occur in two contexts only: as a command, and as the right side of an assign command, declaration preamble, or definition item.

When used as a command, the operation must not return a result. If the operation call terminates normally then the command also terminates normally with no returned value. If the operation call terminates abnormally then so does the command, again with no returned value.

When used in an assign command or a declaration or definition preamble, the operation must return a result of the appropriate type. If the operation call terminates normally then the result is taken as the value of the call; if the call terminates abnormally then so does the assign command or preamble, with the result as the returned value.

8.4 Operations – Operation calls

8.4.3 Examples

The operation *ADD-VALUE* of section 8.2.3 or 8.3.3 must be called in an assign command or a declaration or definition preamble. If it were of no interest whether the effect was an overwrite or an addition, then the result could be ignored:

$MERGE1 : Key \xleftrightarrow{m} \mathbb{N} \xrightarrow{o} ( )$
$MERGE1(db)$
    ext wr *DATABASE* : $Key \xleftrightarrow{m} Value$ $\triangle$
    (**dcl** *x* : OVERWRITE | ADD;
    for $k \in$ **dom** *db* **do** *x* := *ADD-VALUE(k, db(k))*)

On the other hand, the result could be used to keep a count of the number of new records added:

$MERGE2 : Key \xleftrightarrow{m} \mathbb{N} \xrightarrow{o} ( )$
$MERGE2(db)$
    ext wr *DATABASE* : $Key \xleftrightarrow{m} Value$ $\triangle$
(**dcl** *adds* : $\mathbb{N}$:= 0;
    for $k \in$ **dom** *db* **do**
    (**dcl** *res* : ADD | OVERWRITE := *ADD-VALUE(k, db(k))*;
      if *res* = ADD **then** *adds* := *adds* + 1 **else skip**
    );
    return *adds*
)

The form with **using** Sd is needed if the operation Op is defined in a different module to that containing the assign command (see chapter 10). If the state definition associated with the operation definition is to be used (as is usually the case) then **using** Sd is not needed, though it could be used to use a local version of the state introduced by a declaration preamble.

9 Statements

9.1 General

Statements may be used only in explicit operation definitions. Although they have the appearance of programming language statements, they are no less abstract than the rest of VDM-SL; however their meanings are most easily described informally in operational terms, as though they were executed by an abstract machine. Proofs involving statements generally involve consideration of intermediate states, and so are less straightforward than proofs involving only expressions. On the other hand, operations defined explicitly by statements are likely to be closer to an implementation in a conventional programming language.

The basic constructs from which statements are built are called *commands*. A command may affect the values of state and local variables. A command may terminate *normally* or *abnormally*, and may or may not return a value (of any flat type) called the *returned value*. Abnormal termination is intended to be used to indicate an error or exceptional situation. Commands can be aggregated in various ways described in this chapter.

The execution of some compound commands is illustrated by flow diagrams, in which the outer box represents the effect of the entire compound command. Termination is represented by arrows labelled with "exit E" or "rtn E" for abnormal or normal termination respectively with value E; "exit" or "rtn" for termination with no return value; and "exit [E]" or "rtn [E]" for termination with or without a return value.

The following operation illustrates several kinds of commands. It specifies a possible algorithm to implement the *GET-CHANGE* operation of Appendix C.1: it returns as change coins from the current *TAKINGS* equal in value to *BALANCE*, if possible. It implements a greedy algorithm, using as many as possible of the coins under consideration at each stage. This approach is straightforward, but it may fail even though suitable change is available, for example when *BALANCE* is 6p and *TAKINGS* is one 5p and three 2p coins. For this operation the type *Cash* is a multiset of *Coin*, with instantiated functions; see section 7.5.

143

9.1 Statements – General

$GET\text{-}CHANGE\text{-}2 : (\,) \rightarrow Cash$
GET-CHANGE-2( )
ext wr $BALANCE : Money$
$\qquad TAKINGS : Cash$ $\triangleq$
(**dcl** $change : Cash := \{ \mapsto \}$;
  for $coin$ **in** [FIFTY,TWENTY,TEN,FIVE,TWO,ONE] **do**
  (**def** $x = BALANCE$ **div** $WORTH(coin)$,
        $y = num\text{-}cash(TAKINGS, coin)$,
        $z =$ **if** $x<y$ **then** x **else** y **in**
    if $z > 0$ **then**
    ($change := change \cup \{coin \mapsto z\}$;
      $BALANCE := BALANCE - z \times WORTH(coin)$;
      $TAKINGS := diff\text{-}cash(TAKINGS, coin, z)$
)
    else skip
) ;
  if $BALANCE \neq 0$ **then**
  ($BALANCE := BALANCE + WORTH(change)$;
    $TAKINGS := merge\text{-}cash(TAKINGS, change)$;
    $change := \{ \mapsto \}$
)
  else skip;
  return $change$
)

9.2 Commands and bind preambles

9.2.1 Syntax

statement = single statement | block statement;

single statement = [handler, 'in'], {bind preamble}, command;

bind preamble = declaration preamble | definition preamble | let preamble | let be preamble;

command = block statement | assign command
  | nondeterministic command | sequence loop | set loop | indexed loop
  | while loop | call command | McCarthy command
  | if command | cases command | return command
  | exit command | error command | identity command;

block statement = '(', single statement, {';', command}, ')';

identity command = 'skip';

error command = 'error';

declaration preamble = 'dcl', declaration item, ';';

declaration item = identifier, ':', type expression, [':=', expression]
  | identifier, ':', type expression, [':=', operation call];

definition preamble = 'def', definition item, {',', definition item}, ';';

definition item = pattern or bind, '=', expression
  | pattern or bind, '=', operation call;

let preamble = 'let', pattern or bind, '=', expression,
  {',', pattern or bind, '=', expression}, 'in';

let be preamble = 'let', bind, ['be', 'st', expression], 'in';

9.2.2 Meaning

The body of an explicitly defined operation is a *statement*; this is essentially a sequence of *commands* separated by semicolons and surrounded by parentheses; the commands are executed in order from the beginning.

The commands of a statement can be headed by a *handler* and/or one or more *bind preambles*. A handler traps certain termination conditions of the statement; a bind preamble introduces local declarations with the rest of the statement as scope.

9.2 Statements – Commands and bind preambles

A statement containing only one command may have the surrounding parentheses omitted, when it is called a *single statement*; if the parentheses are present the statement is called a *block statement*. A block statement (but not a single statement) counts as a command, so that statements may be nested.

The commands in a statement are executed in order until a return or exit statement is executed, a command terminates abnormally or normally with a returned value, or the sequence is exhausted (see Figure 1). In the last two cases, the returned value and termination condition of the statement are those of the last command executed, though this may be modified by a handler: see section 9.3.

An *identity command* has the form:

skip

It has no effect, always terminates normally, and returns no value.

An *error command* has the form:

error

This is equivalent to:

return undefined

(see section 7.3); it implicitly extends the precondition of the operation containing it to exclude any values of parameters and state variables which cause an attempt to execute it.

The *bind preambles* declare identifiers local to the statement. There are four forms.

A *declaration preamble* has one of the forms:

dcl Id : T := E;
dcl Id : T;

where Id is an identifier, T is a type expression, and E is an expression of type T or an operation call to an operation returning a result of type T. The effect is to declare a local variable Id of type T, with scope the following part of the enclosing statement. If E is given, it is evaluated and assigned as an initial value to Id. E can contain state variables and local

9.2 Statements – Commands and bind preambles

variables introduced earlier by a declaration preamble. If E is an operation call which terminates abnormally, execution of the current statement is terminated abnormally with the result returned by the operation as returned value (see Figure 1). Local variables can be read and written to in the same way as state variables, but exist only during execution of the enclosing statement.

A *definition preamble* has the form:

> **def** $Pb_1 = E_1$,
> $\qquad\;\;Pb_2 = E_2$,
> $\qquad\;\;...$
> $\qquad\;\;Pb_n = E_n$;

where each Pb_i is a pattern Pt_i, a set bind $Pt_i \in S_i$, or a type bind $Pt_i : T_i$, and each E_i is an expression or operation call. As with a declaration preamble, the E_i may contain state and local variables, as may the patterns Pt_i (in match values) and the set expressions S_i). The type T_i or set S_i, if given, constrains the value of E_i to be of that type or an element of that set. Each expression or operation call E_i is evaluated in turn and matched to the corresponding pattern Pt_i; the bindings from that matching are effective for the scope of the pattern identifiers, that is the following part of the preamble and the enclosing statement. If any E_i is an operation call which terminates abnormally, execution of the statement is terminated abnormally with the result returned by the operation (see Figure 1). If any E_i fails to match, the definition preamble is invalid. The above definition preamble is equivalent to the sequence of definition preambles:

> **def** $Pb_1 = E_1$;
> **def** $Pb_2 = E_2$;
> $\qquad\;\;...$
> **def** $Pb_n = E_n$;

A *let preamble* has the form:

> **let** $Pb_1 = E_1$,
> $\qquad\;\;Pb_2 = E_2$,
> $\qquad\;\;...$
> $\qquad\;\;Pb_n = E_n$ **in**

9.2 Statements – Commands and bind preambles

where each Pb_i is a pattern Pt_i, a set bind $Pt_i \in S_i$, or a type bind $Pt_i : T_i$, and each E_i is an expression. This is similar to the corresponding definition preamble except that the E_i, the Pt_i, and the S_i cannot contain variables, and the E_i cannot be operation calls, and so cannot affect the values of variables; and all the patterns Pt_i are matched to the values of the corresponding expressions E_i at the same time. The scope of the pattern identifiers in the Pt_i is the following part of the enclosing statement, after the **in**. If no set of matchings can be found, the preamble is invalid.

A *let be preamble* has one of the forms:

  let Bd **be st** B **in**
  let Bd **in**

where Bd is a set bind Pt ∈ S or a type bind Pt : T, and B is a Boolean expression involving the pattern identifiers of Pt. B is optional; the default is **true**. The pattern Pt is matched to a value of type T or elements of the set S for which B is **true**; if there is more than one such value, one is chosen nondeterministically. If no such matching is possible, the preamble is invalid. The pattern Pt and the set expression S must not contain any variables. The scope of the pattern identifiers in Pt is the following part of the enclosing statement.

9.2.3 Examples

The identity command is useful where the syntax demands a command, as in a conditional command:

  if *alarm* **then** *panic*( ) **else skip**

An operational form of the depth function of section 7.3.3, which finds the maximum depth of nesting of parentheses in an expression, illustrates the use of declaration preambles and the error command.

  $DEPTH : \mathbb{N} \times \mathbb{N} \times \mathbf{char}^* \xrightarrow{o} \mathbb{N}$

  $DEPTH(max, count, str) \triangleq$
  (**dcl** $x : \mathbb{N}$;
     if card $str = 0$ **then**
        if $count \neq 0$ **then error else return** max

9.2 Statements – Commands and bind preambles

```
     else
      (  cases hd exp in
         ('(')  →  x := DEPTH(max, count + 1, tl exp),
         (')')  →
             if count < 1 then error
             else x := DEPTH(if count > max then count else max,
                  count - 1, tl exp),
         others  →  x := DEPTH(max, count, tl exp)
         end;
     return x
)
```

9.2 Statements – Commands and bind preambles

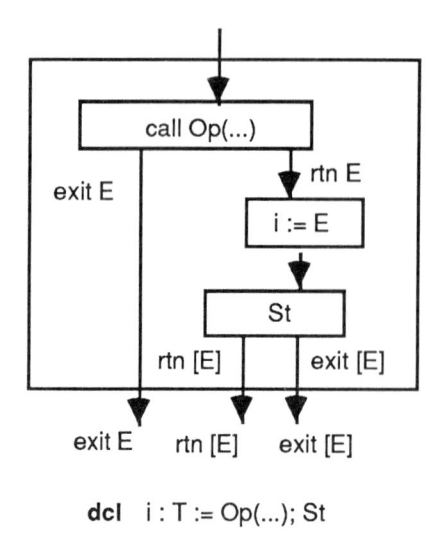

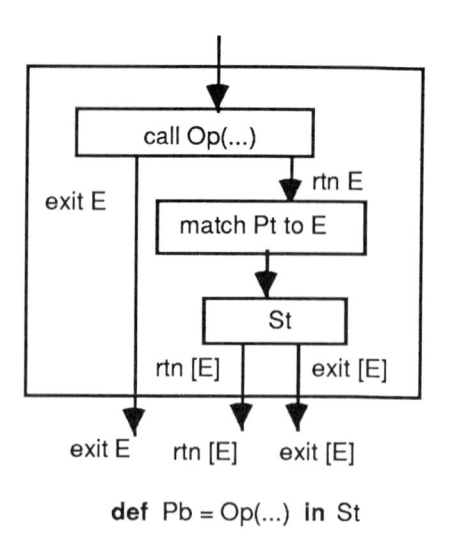

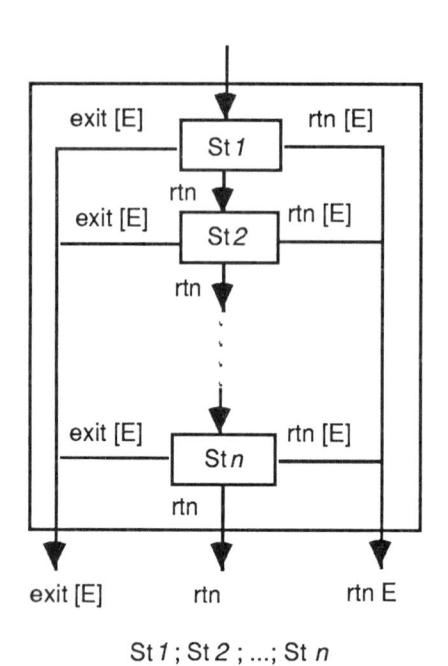

dcl i : T := Op(...); St

def Pb = Op(...) **in** St

St 1; St 2 ; ...; St n

Figure 1   Operation calls in bind preambles and statement sequencing

150

9.3 Handlers

9.3.1 Syntax

   handler= always handler | nonrecursive handler | recursive handler;

   always handler = **'always'**, statement;

   nonrecursive handler = **'trap'**, pattern or bind, **'with'**, statement;

   recursive handler = **'tixe'**, trap definition list;

   trap definition list = '{', pattern or bind, '↦', statement, {',', pattern or bind, '↦', statement}, '}';

   return command = **'return'**, [expression];

   exit command = **'exit'**, [expression];

9.3.2 Meaning

A *handler* prescribes how certain termination conditions of the statement it heads are to be treated.

- If there is an *always handler*, with the form:

    always St

    where St is a statement, any termination of the statement is trapped and results in execution of the statement St. If St terminates abnormally, then the enclosing statement terminates abnormally with the same returned value if any. If St terminates normally, then the enclosing statement terminates in the same way as the statement governed by the handler, and with the same returned value if any.

- With a *nonrecursive handler*, which has the form:

    trap Pb **with** St

    where Pb is a pattern Pt, a set bind Pt ∈ S, or a type bind Pt : T, any abnormal termination of the statement is trapped. If there is a returned value which matches Pt, and which is an element of S or a member of T if given, then the statement St is executed. The enclosing statement terminates normally or abnormally according as St does, and with the same returned value, if any. If there is no

151

9.3 Statements – Handlers

returned value, or one which does not match Pt, then the enclosing statement terminates abnormally with the returned value unchanged, as though the handler had been absent.

- With a *recursive handler*, which has the form:

  tixe $Pb_1 \mapsto St_1, Pb_2 \mapsto St_2, ..., Pb_n \mapsto St_n$,

  where the each Pb_i is a pattern Pt_i, a set bind $Pt_i \in S_i$, or a type bind $Pt_i : T_i$, and the St_i are statements, any abnormal termination of the enclosing statement is trapped. If a value is returned it is matched against the patterns Pt_i; if any match is found, the corresponding statement St_i is executed. If no value is returned, or no match is found, the statement is terminated abnormally with the returned value unchanged, as if the handler were absent. If more than one match is found, one is chosen nondeterministically. If the statement St_i terminates normally, the enclosing statement terminates normally with the value returned by St_i, if any; otherwise the whole process is repeated as if the termination was of the enclosing statement. This process must terminate or the handler is invalid. ("Tixe" is "exit" backwards, as a recursive handler is in a sense the terminator of an exit statement.)

The execution of handlers is illustrated in Figure 2. The scope of any pattern identifiers in the pattern Pt of a nonrecursive handler is the statement St. The scope of any pattern identifiers in a pattern Pt_i in a recursive handler is the corresponding statement St_i.

The use of a bind instead of a pattern Pt_i in a handler limits the choice of matching value to the type or set of the bind; see section 6.2.

A *return command* has one of the forms:

    return E   **return**

where E is an expression. It terminates execution of the enclosing statement normally, returning the value of E. If E is omitted, no value is returned.

An *exit command* has one of the forms:

    exit E   **exit**

where E is an expression. It terminates execution of the enclosing statement abnormally, returning the value of E. If E is omitted, no value is returned.

9.3.3 Examples

Handlers in explicit operation definitions play a rôle similar to that of error definitions in implicit operations, in that they allow exceptional or erroneous conditions to be dealt with. An explicit version of the operation *GET-DRINK* of section 8.2.3 might be as follows, where *DISPLAY* is an operation which displays an appropriate message to the user.

GET-DRINK-EXP : *Drink* $\xrightarrow{o}$ [*Drink*]

GET-DRINK-EXP(*choice*) ≙
(**trap** *err* **with** (*DISPLAY*(*err*); **return nil**;
   if $\exists\, i \in$ *INGREDIENTS* (*choice*) · *STOCKS*(*i*) = 0
   then exit LOW-STOCK
   elseif *CUPS* = 0
   then exit NO-CUPS
   elseif *BALANCE* < *PRICES*(*choice*)
   then exit MORE-MONEY
   else
   (*BALANCE* := *BALANCE* − *PRICES*(*choice*);
      CUPS := *CUPS* − 1;
      STOCKS := *STOCKS* † {*i* ↦ *STOCKS*(*i*) − 1
          | *i* ∈ *INGREDIENTS*(*choice*)};
      return *choice*
)
)

The recursive handler was invented to model the effect of **goto** statements in programming languages (since a **goto** statement can lead to another **goto** statement). As an illustration of its other uses, consider the following version of the operation *DEPTH* of section 9.2.3, which returns the maximum depth of parenthesis nesting in an expression. The recursive handler is used to handle the error condition of an unbalanced ')' by adding a '(' at the front of the expression and trying again. The error condition of an unbalanced '(' is trapped but no attempt is made here at error correction: the operation just terminates abnormally with the result found. Quote values are used as the returned values to avoid trapping this last exit.

9.3 Statements – Handlers

$DEPTH : \textbf{char}^* \xrightarrow{o} \mathbb{N}$

$DEPTH(exp) \triangleq$
(**dcl** $count : \mathbb{N} := 0, max : \mathbb{N} := 0$;
  tixe {(ERR1) $\mapsto$
      (**dcl** $max : \mathbb{N}$; $max := DEPTH(\text{"("} \frown exp)$; **exit** max),
      (ERR2) $\mapsto$ **exit** max} **in**
  (**for** $i = 1$ **to len** exp **do**
     cases $exp(i)$ **in**
     ('(') $\rightarrow$ $c := 1$,
     (')') $\rightarrow$
        (**if** $c > max$ **then** $max := c$ **else skip**;
          $c := c - 1$;
          if $c < 0$ **then exit** ERR1 **else skip**
)
     end;
    if $c \neq 0$ **then exit** ERR2 **else return** max
)
)

9.3 Statements – Handlers

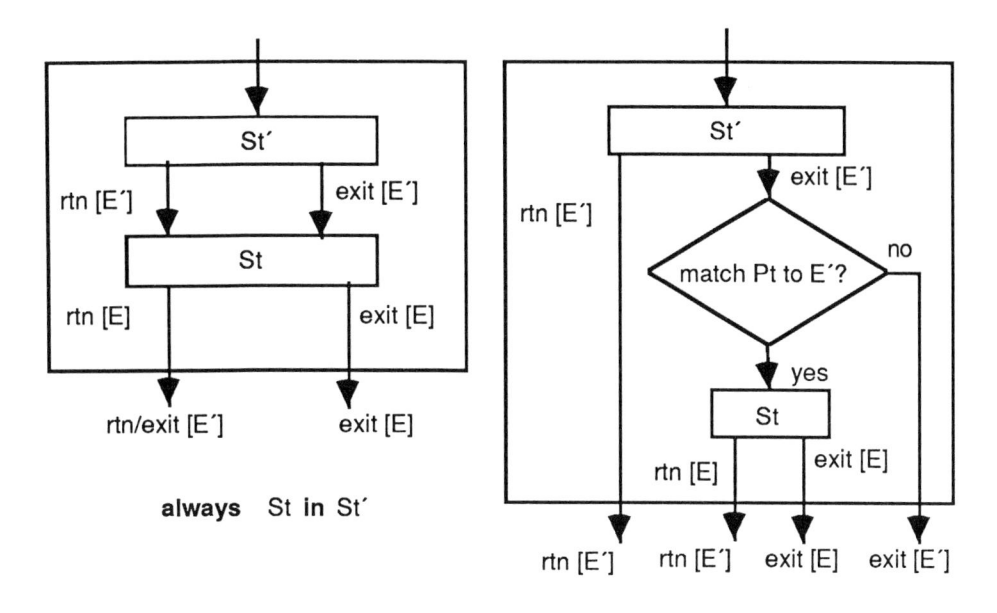

always St **in** St′

trap Pb **with** St **in** St′

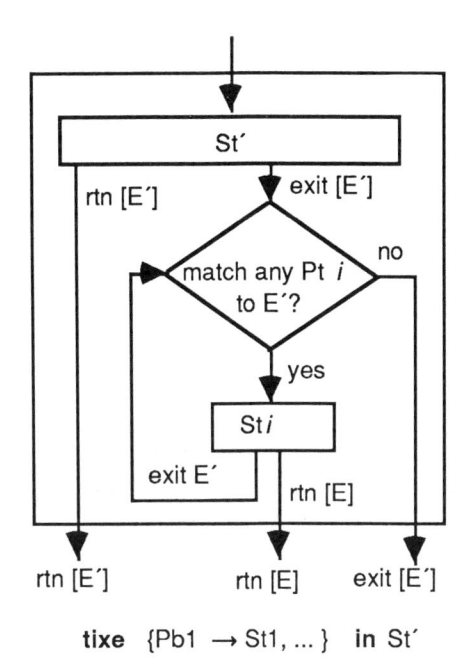

tixe {Pb1 → St1, ... } **in** St′

Figure 2 Handlers

9.4 Assign commands

9.4.1 Syntax

assign command = state designator, ':=', expression
| state designator, ':=', operation call;

state designator = name | field reference | map reference
| sequence reference;

field reference = state designator, '.', identifier;

map reference = state designator, '(', expression, ')';

sequence reference = state designator, '(', expression, ')';

9.4.2 Meaning

An *assign command* has one of two forms. The first is:

Sd := E

where Sd is a state designator and E is an expression of the same type as Sd. It assigns the value of E to the state or local variable, or component of one of these, denoted by Sd, and terminates normally with no returned value. The value of E must be of the type of Sd.

The second form is one of:

Sd := Op(E_1, E_2, ..., E_n)
Sd := Op(E_1, E_2, ..., E_n) **using** Sd_2

where Sd is as for the first form, and the right side is a call to operation Op with actual parameters E_i (see section 8.4) returning a result of the type of Sd. For Sd_2 see section 8.4. The effect is to execute the operation call; if it terminates normally, the result (which must be of the type of Sd) is assigned to Sd, and the assignment command terminates normally with no returned value. If the operation call terminates abnormally, Sd is unchanged and the assignment command terminates abnormally with the same returned value. See Figure 3.

A *state designator* Sd which is a name denotes the variable with that name. In the flat language, a name is just an identifier; for other possibilities see chapter 10. The variable may be a state variable or a local variable introduced by a declaration preamble. The other forms denote components of variables as follows:

9.4 Statements – Assign commands

- *field reference* Sd´.Id: the field Id of the record denoted by Sd´;

- *map reference* Sd´(E´): the element of the range of the map denoted by Sd´ corresponding to the domain element E´;

- *sequence reference* Sd´(E´): the element of the sequence denoted by Sd´ corresponding to the index E´.

If Sd is a map reference or sequence reference Sd´(E´), then the value of E´ must be in the domain or the index set respectively of Sd´.

9.4.3 Examples

In the vending machine specification of Appendix C.1, the state contains a map *STOCKS* from ingredients to natural numbers. An assignment command to decrement the stock of tea is:

STOCKS(TEA) := *STOCKS*(TEA) - 1

where on the left side *STOCKS*(TEA) is a state designator and on the right side it is an expression. In some dialects, but not in VDM-SL, there is an explicit *contents operator* which must be applied to a state designator to yield its value; in VDM-SL the contents operator is implicit.

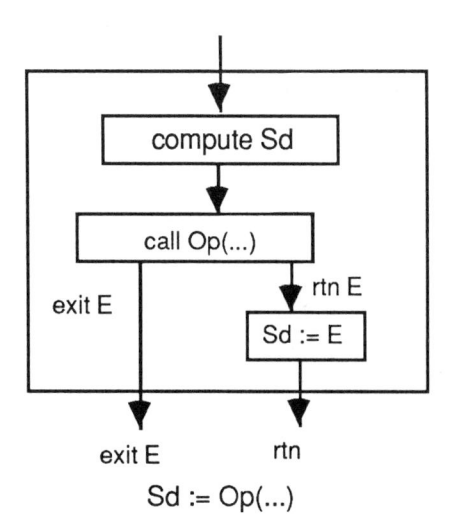

Figure 3 Operation calls in assign commands

9.5 Nondeterministic commands

9.5.1 Syntax

nondeterministic command = '||', '(', statement, {',', statement}, ')';

9.5.2 Meaning

A *nondeterministic command* has the form:

$$||(St_1, St_2, ..., St_n)$$

and represents the "parallel" execution of the component statements St_1, St_2, ..., St_n. In fact the effect is as if the St_i are executed in a nondeterministically chosen order; it is the same as:

$$St_1'; St_2'; ...; St_n'$$

where the St_j' are a permutation of the St_i.

9.5.3 Examples

A nondeterministic command is useful when the order of execution of a number of commands affects the outcome in a way that is not of interest at the present level of abstraction. For example, the following operation assembles the ingredients for a drink without specifying the order, though that may have a detectable effect on the result (see Appendix C.1).

    MAKE-DRINK : *Drink* $\xrightarrow{o}$ ( )
    MAKE-DRINK (*d*) ≙
        cases *d* **in**
        mk-Tea-or-coffee (*tc*, *wh*, *sw*) →
            ||(**if** *tc* = TEA **then** *ADD*(TEA) **else** *ADD*(COFFEE),
                if *wh* **then** *ADD*(MILK) **else** **skip**,
                if *sw* **then** *ADD*(SUGAR) **else** **skip**
            ),
        CHOCOLATE → *ADD*(CHOCOLATE)
        end

If the effect is independent of the order then there is no need to use a nondeterministic command.

9.5 Statements – Nondeterministic commands

The component commands are not executed simultaneously; thus:

$||(x := y, y := x)$

results in x and y having the same value, either the previous value of x or that of y. Similarly:

$||(x := 0, x := 1)$

results in x having the value 0 or the value 1.

9.6 Loops

9.6.1 Syntax

   sequence loop = **'for'**, pattern or bind, **'in'**, [**'reverse'**], expression, **'do'**, statement;

   set loop = **'for'**, **'all'**, pattern, **'ε'**, expression, **'do'**, statement;

   indexed loop = **'for'**, identifier, **'='**, expression, **'to'**, expression, [**'by'**, expression], **'do'**, statement;

   while loop = **'while'**, expression, **'do'**, statement;

9.6.2 Meaning

A *loop* repeatedly executes a component statement. In each case the context may be changed by the execution of the statement; apart from such changes the sequence of contexts is as described below.

A *sequence loop* has the form:

   for Pb **in** Q **do** St

where Pb is a pattern Pt, a type bind Pt : T, or a set bind Pt ε S, and Q is a sequence. The contexts are given by matching the pattern Pt to each element Q(1), Q(2), ..., Q(**len** Q) of Q in turn; the expression Q is evaluated before the matching takes place. If **reverse** is present, the order of contexts is reversed. The use of a bind instead of a pattern constrains the values of Q(*i*) to be of type T or elements of the set S. Each match must succeed, or the command is invalid.

If Q is the empty sequence, the loop is equivalent to **skip**. If any iteration terminates abnormally, then the entire loop command terminates abnormally at that point with the same returned value, if any. If any iteration terminates normally but returns a result (for example by executing a return command) then the entire loop terminates normally with the same returned value.

A *set loop* has the form:

   for all Pt ε S **do** St

160

9.6 Statements – Loops

where Pt is a pattern, S is a set, and St is a statement. The contexts are given by matching Pt to each element of S in a nondeterministically chosen order. For that order the effect is as for a sequence loop, so that the above set loop is equivalent to the sequence loop:

> **for** Pt **in** (E_1, E_2, ..., E_n) **do** St

where S = {E_1, E_2, ..., E_n}. The set expression S is evaluated before any matching takes place.

An *indexed loop* has the form:

> **for** Id = E_1 **to** E_2 **by** E_3 **do** St

where Id is an identifier, E_1, E_2, and E_3 are expressions, and St is a statement. The contexts are given by binding Id to the numeric values E_1, $E_1 + E_3$, $E_1 + 2 \times E_3$, ..., $E_1 + n \times E_3$ where n = **floor**(($E_2 - E_1$)/E_3), that is the largest non-negative integer for which the value does not go beyond E_2. If **by** E_3 is omitted, the default value of E_3 is 1. If $E_1 - E_2$ and E_3 are both positive or both negative, then the entire loop is equivalent to **skip**. E_1, E_2, and E_3 are evaluated once only, before the first iteration. E_3 must not be 0.

The scope of any pattern identifiers in the pattern Pt of a sequence or set loop, and of the index identifier Id in an indexed loop, is the statement St. An indexed loop declares the index identifier Id.

A *while loop* has the form:

> **while** B **do** St

where B is a Boolean expression and St is a statement. The effect is as follows. B is evaluated; if it is **false**, then the loop terminates normally with no returned value. If B is **true**, then the statement St is executed; if it terminates abnormally, or normally with a returned value, then the entire loop terminates in the same way and with the same returned value. Otherwise the process is repeated from the evaluation of B.

All loops must terminate. A sequence, set, or indexed loop always terminates if the statement St always does. A while loop terminates only if at some point the value of B is **false**, or the statement St terminates abnormally or with a returned value; this often needs to be proved. The execution of loops is illustrated in Figure 4.

9.6 Statements – Loops

9.6.3 Examples

The following all have largely the same effect; note that only the while loop needs a separate declaration for the variable *i*.

    for *i* **in** [1, ..., **len** A] **do** A[*i*] := 0
    for all *i* ∈ **inds** A **do** A[*i*] := 0
    for *i* = 1 **to len** A **do** A[*i*] := 0
    dcl *i* : $\mathbb{N}$; *i* := 1; **while** *i* ≤ **len** A **do** (A[*i*] := 0; *i* := *i*+1)

As a simple example of a termination proof, consider the following variation on the change-giving algorithm of section 9.1. This version takes coins at random until the change is complete or it sticks; only the inner loop is given.

    while ∃ *c* ∈ **dom** *TAKINGS* · *WORTH*(*c*) ≤ *BALANCE* **do**
        let *c* ∈ **dom** *TAKINGS* **be st** *WORTH*(*c*) ≤ *BALANCE* **in**
        (*BALANCE* := *BALANCE* − *WORTH*(*c*);
         TAKINGS := *remove*(*TAKINGS*, *c*))

To show termination, it is only necessary to note that *BALANCE* is non-negative, and is decreased by each iteration; and certainly the loop terminates if *BALANCE* is 0 (as no coin is worthless, the existential quantification is then **false**). This is a frequently useful technique.

9.6 Statements – Loops

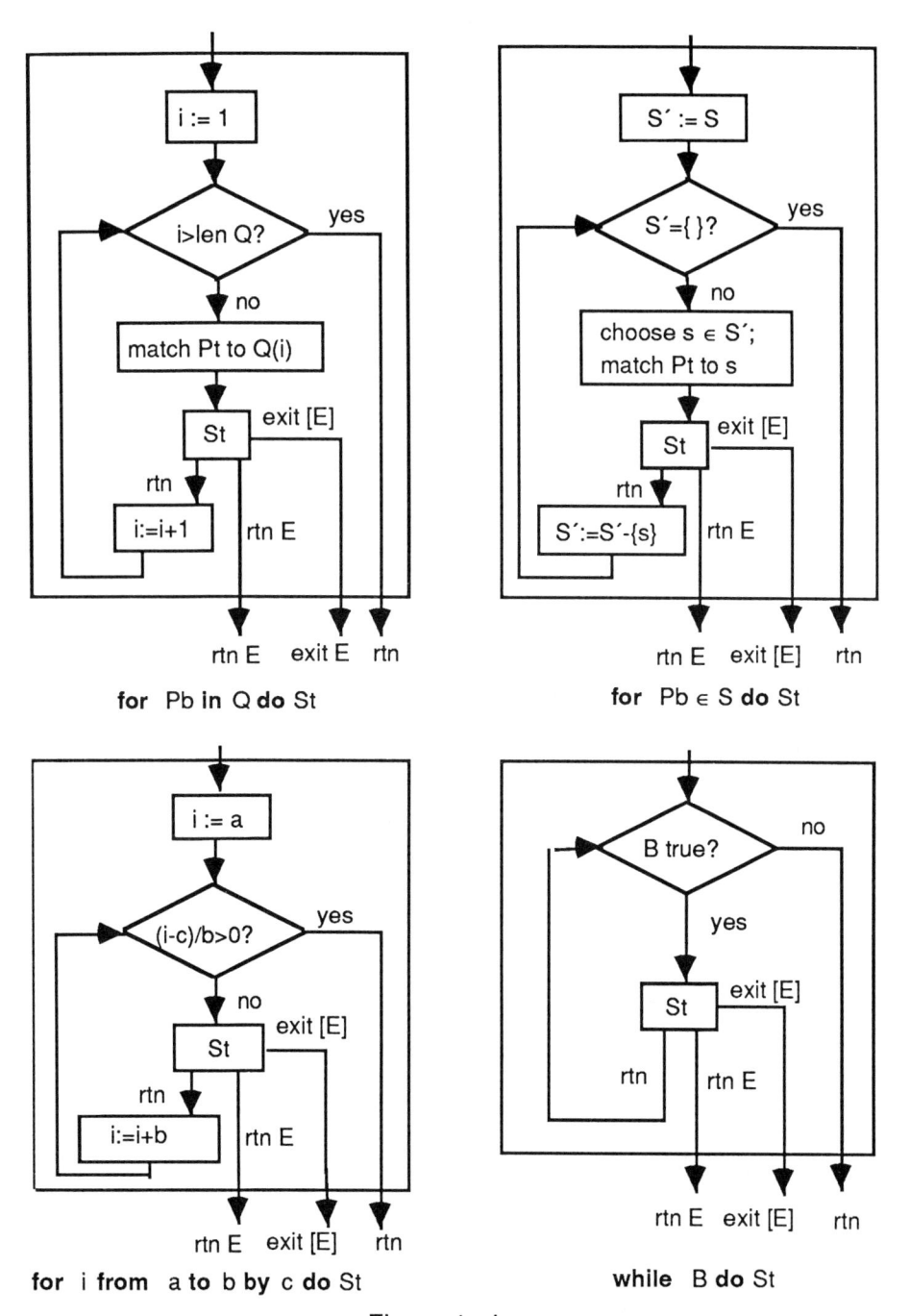

Figure 4   Loops

9.7 Conditional commands

9.7.1 Syntax

    if command = **'if'**, expression, **'then'**, statement, {elseif command clause}, **'else'**, statement;

    elseif command clause = **'elseif'**, expression, **'then'**, statement;

    McCarthy command = '(', guarded statement list, [',', others command choice], ')';

    guarded statement list = expression, '→', statement, {',', expression, '→', statement};

    others command choice = **'others'**, '→', statement;

    cases command = **'cases'**, expression, ':', command choice list, [',', others command choice], **'end'**;

    command choice list = command choice, {',', command choice};

    command choice = pattern list, '→', statement;

9.7.2 Meaning

Conditional commands allow statements to be executed conditionally, or one of several statements to be chosen for execution.

An *if command* has the form:

    if B **then** St_1 **else** St_2

where B is a Boolean expression and St_1 and St_2 are statements. It is equivalent to St_1 if B is **true** and to St_2 if B is **false**. If elseif command clauses are present:

    if B_1 **then** St_1
    elseif B_2 **then** St_2
    ...
    elseif B_n **then** St_n
    else St

the effect is the same as:

9.7 Statements – Conditional commands

```
if B₁ then St₁
else (if B₂ then St₂
    else (...
        else (if Bₙ then Stₙ
            else St)...))
```

The first St_i for which B_i is **true** is executed, or St if none is.

A *cases command* has the form:

```
cases E:
    Pt₁,₁, Pt₁,₂, ... → St₁,
    Pt₂,₁, Pt₂,₂, ... → St₂,
    ...,
    Ptₙ,₁, Ptₙ,₂, ... → Stₙ,
    others → St
end
```

where the $Pt_{i,j}$ are patterns, the St_i are statements, and E is an expression. The effect is that the choices $Pt_{i,1}, Pt_{i,2}, ... \to St_i$ are taken in order for $i = 1, ..., n$, and all the patterns $Pt_{i,j}$ are matched to the value of E for each chopice until one is found with a pattern $Pt_{i,j}$ which matches the value of E. When that happens the statement St_i is executed in the context of the bindings from that match. If more than one pattern in a choice matches E, one is chosen nondeterministically. If no pattern $Pt_{i,j}$ matches E, then the statement St in the others choice is executed; if no others command choice is supplied in such a case then the cases command is invalid.

The scope of any pattern identifiers in each pattern $Pt_{i,j}$ is the corresponding statement St_i.

A *McCarthy command* has one of the the forms:

$(E_1 \to St_1, E_2 \to St_2, ..., E_n \to St_n,$ **others** $\to St)$
$(E_1 \to St_1, E_2 \to St_2, ..., E_n \to St_n)$

where the E_i are expressions and the St_i and St are statements. It has exactly the same meaning as the if command:

165

9.7 Statements – Conditional commands

> if E_1 then St_1
> elseif E_2 then St_2
> ...
> elseif E_n then St_n
> else St

where St is replaced by **skip** in the second case.

9.7.3 Examples

The remarks of section 6.5.3 on the use of elseif clauses and nested if expressions apply equally to is commands. The use of a McCarthy command instead of an if command is entirely a matter of taste.

As an example of overlapping choices, consider the cases command:

> **cases** *str* **in**
>   *str1* ̂ "XXX" ̂ *str2* → *str* := *str1* ̂ *str2* ,
>   *str1* ̂ "XX" ̂ *str2* → *str* := *str1* ̂ *str2* ,
>   *str1* ̂ "X" ̂ *str2* → *str* := *str1* ̂ *str2*
> **end**

which removes a block of up to 3 consecutive 'X's from *str*. If the choices were reversed, only the first would ever be selected.

10 Modules

10.1 Module interfaces and bodies

10.1.1 Syntax

document = module list | definition block list;

module list = module, {module};

module = '**module**', identifier, interface part, [definition part], '**end**', identifier;

definition part = '**definitions**', definition block list;

interface part = [module parameter section], [module import section], [module instantiation section], [module export section];

module signature = signature block, {signature block};

signature block = type signature block | value signature block | function signature block | operation signature block;

type signature block = '**types**', type description, {';', type description};

type description = name | type definition;

value signature block = '**values**', value description, {';', value description};

value description = name list, ':', type expression;

function signature block = '**functions**', function signature, {';', function signature};

function signature = name list, ':', function type expression;

operation signature block = '**operations**', operation signature, {';', operation signature};

operation signature = name list, ':', operation type expression, ['**using**', name];

definition block list = definition block, {definition block};

10.1 Modules – Module interfaces and bodies

```
definition block = type definition block | state definition
     | value definition block | function definition block
     | operation definition block;
```

10.1.2 Meaning

A *module list* is a sequence of one or more modules, a module being a fairly self-contained unit with an identifier, an interface defining the external properties of the module, and a set of definitions.

A *module* has the form

> **module** Id
>   interface part
>   definition part
> **end** Id

The same identifier Id must occur at the beginning and end of a module.

The *interface part* defines the external properties of the module. It consists of four parts. The *module export section* and the *module import section* control the visibility of names of entities in other modules; see section 10.2. The *module parameter section* and *module instantiation section* allow parameterized modules to be written and to be instantiated with specific values; see section 10.3.

The entities exported from a module are defined by the *definition part*, consisting of definitions preceded by the keyword **definitions** and arranged in *definition blocks*, each containing definitions of a particular kind of entity (types, values, functions, operations, or state variables) and introduced by an appropriate keyword. There can be any number (including none) of definition blocks of each kind, in any order, but a definition block list must be at least one definition block of some kind. A module need have no definition part at all, for example if all the exported entities are explicit types and values. Definitions are described further in the appropriate sections. All identifiers of defined entities must be different.

The interface properties of a module are all expressed in terms of *module signatures*: sequences of descriptions of types, values, functions, and operations, arranged like definitions in blocks (each called a *signature block*) according to kind. Each description identifies an entity to be exported or imported, or a formal parameter of a parameterized module.

10.1 Modules – Module interfaces and bodies

A *type description* is either the name of a type or a full type definition; the latter exports or imports the details as well as the name of the type definition.

Value descriptions, *function signatures*, and *operation signatures* are lists of names of values, functions, and operations and their types. An operation signature in an module export section can also have a *using clause*: **using** followed by the name of the state on which the operation operates. If the operation is defined in the current module and the state has the same name as the module, the using clause may be omitted.

10.1.3 Examples

Suppose the vending machine specified in section 1.3 were to be considered as one part of a larger system, an automated cafeteria perhaps. It could then be written as a module representing a vending machine in the abstract (as an abstract data type):

> **module** *Vending-Machine*-1
>   **definitions**
>   **types**
>   ...
>   **state**
>   ...
>   **operations**
>   ...
> **end** *Vending-Machine*-1

Here, as is usual though not essential, the module name is the same as the name of the state.

As this module has no interface, it is not yet very useful as a component of a larger specification. This is remedied in section 10.2.3.

10.2 Import and export

10.2.1 Syntax

module import section = **'imports'**, import definition,
{',', import definition};

import definition = **'from'**, identifier, module signature;

module export section = **'exports'**, module signature;

10.2.2 Meaning

A *module import section* has the form:

imports
   from Id_1 Ms_1,
   from Id_2 Ms_2,
   ...
   from Id_n Ms_n,

where each Id_i is the identifier of a non-parameterized module in the same document and Ms_i is a module signature containing descriptions of entities from the export section of the module Id_i. For a value, function, or operation, the corresponding type must be the same. The names in the Ms_i may be used in the export section, instantiation section, and definition part of the enclosing module. The import section identifies entities exported from other modules which are used in this one.

A *module export section* has the form:

   exports Ms

where Ms is a module signature containing descriptions of entities defined in the current module or imported into the module in an import definition or in an instantiation instance (see section 10.3). This identifies the entities exported from the module, that is, the entities which are importable into other modules. In the case of types, either the whole type definition may be exported or just the name; this is the only place that a type description which is a type definition can occur in a module signature. For a value, function, or operation, the corresponding type must be the same. The names in Ms may be used in the module export section of every other module in the same document.

10.2 Modules – Import and export

It is not allowed for two or more modules to import from each other: the graph of imports must be acyclic.

10.2.3 Examples

To embed the vending machine module of section 10.1.3 in a larger specification, it must export its operations and the types and values needed to call them. At the same time, another module could be written to take care of operations on *Money*, likely to be needed for other parts of the specification. This can also hide the information that *Money* is just $\mathbb{N}$ by putting only the name *Money* in the export list, so preventing abuse of the type for example by multiplying two sums of money together.

    module *Vending-Machine*-1
      import from *Fiscal*
        types *Money*
        functions
          add, subtract: *Money* × *Money* → *Money*
      exports
        types *Fiscal* `*Money*, *Drink*
        operations
          INSERT-MONEY: *Money* $\xrightarrow{o}$ ( );
          GET-DRINK: *Drink* $\xrightarrow{o}$ *Drink* × *Money*
    definitions
      state *Vending-Machine*-1 **of**
        BALANCE : *Money*
        PRICES : *Drink* $\xrightarrow{m}$ *Money*
      inv *mk-Vending-Machine*-1(–, c) ≜ ∀ d : *Drink* · d ∈ **dom** c
      init *mk-Vending-Machine*-1(c, –) ≜ c = 0
      operations
        INSERT-MONEY(*cash* : *Money*)
          ext wr *BALANCE* : *Money*
          post *BALANCE* = $\overleftarrow{BALANCE}$ + *cash*;
        GET-DRINK(*choice* : *Drink*) **return** : *Drink*, *change* : *Money*
          ext wr *BALANCE* : *Money*
            rd *PRICES* : *Drink* $\xrightarrow{m}$ *Money*
          pre *BALANCE* ≥ *PRICES*(*choice*)
          post *BALANCE* = 0 ∧ **return** = *choice*
              ∧ *change* = $\overleftarrow{BALANCE}$ – *PRICES*(*choice*)
    end *Vending-Machine*-1

10.2 Modules – Import and export

module *Fiscal*
  exports
    types *Money*
    functions
      add, subtract: *Money* × *Money* → *Money*
  definitions
    types
      Money = $\mathbb{N}$
    functions
      add : *Money* × *Money* → *Money*
      add(*m1*, *m2*) $\triangleq$ *m1* + *m2*;
      subtract : *Money* × *Money* → *Money*
      subtract(*m1*, *m2*) $\triangleq$ *m1* − *m2*
end *Fiscal*

10.3 Parameterized modules

10.3.1 Syntax

module parameter section = **'parameters'**, module signature;

module instantiation section = **'instantiation'**,
    module instantiation, {',', module instantiation};

module instantiation = identifier, **'as'**, module instance;

module instance = identifier, '(', [substitution,
    {',', substitution}], ')', [module signature];

substitution = identifier, '→', name;

10.3.2 Meaning

A *module parameter section* has the form:

parameters Ms

A module with a module parameter section is a *generic* or *parameterized module*, acting as a template. The module parameter section acts as a set of formal parameters to the module, allowing it to be written in a general fashion and instantiated with particular values. As the entities defined in the module export section of a parameterized module depend in general on the module parameter section, they cannot be imported into another module; instead the module must first be instantiated in the module instantiation section of the importing module. A parameterized module can import entities from other, non-parameterized, modules.

A *module instantiation section* has the form:

instantiation
Id_1 **as** $Id_1'(Id_{1,1} \rightarrow Nm_{1,1}, Id_{1,2} \rightarrow Nm_{1,2}, ...) Ms_1$,
Id_2 **as** $Id_2'(Id_{2,1} \rightarrow Nm_{2,1}, Id_{2,2} \rightarrow Nm_{2,2}, ...) Ms_2$,
...,
Id_m **as** $Id_m'(Id_{m,1} \rightarrow Nm_{m,1}, Id_{m,2} \rightarrow Nm_{m,2}, ...) Ms_m$

It defines instances of parameterized modules for use in this module, by supplying the actual module parameters, and imports entities from the instantiated module's module export section. In a module instantiation, the first identifier Id_i gives a new name to the module instance. The second identifier Id_i' is the name of the parameterized module. The

10.3 Modules – Parameterized modules

substitution list gives the actual parameter $Nm_{i,j}$ to be substituted for each module parameter $Id_{i,j}$; and the module signature Ms_i acts as an import definition from the instantiated module. A non-parameterized module can also be instantiated; this just serves to change the name of the module and the exported entities.

Each type, value, function, and operation in the module signature Ms of the module parameter section acts as a declaration of the identifier, with scope the current module interface and body, and the substitution list of any module instance of the module.

In a module instance, an actual module parameter (a type, value, function, or operation, appropriately) must be given for every module parameter of a module which is being instantiated. The same rules apply to the actual parameters as to exports: each actual module parameter must be defined either in an import list (or implicit import list in an instantiation) in the module interface, or in a definition in the definition part of the enclosing module. For a value, function, or operation, the corresponding type must be the same. A type description which is a type definition is not allowed.

Each type, value, function, and operation mentioned in the module signature Ms_i in a module instance must also be mentioned in the export list of the parameterized module Id_i (with the substitutions for the module parameter section having been made). For a value, function or operation the corresponding type must be the same. A type description which is a type definition is not allowed.

The ban on cyclic imports (see section 10.2.2) applies also to importation via instantiation.

10.3.3 Examples

The polymorphic functions of section 7.5 could conveniently be written as a parameterized module with element type as module parameter:

    module *Multiset*
        parameters
            types *elem*
        exports
            types *bag*
            functions
                empty-bag : ( ) → *bag*;
                num-bag : *elem* × *bag* → $\mathbb{N}$;

10.3 Modules – Parameterized modules

      plus-bag : elem × bag → bag;
      mems-bag : bag → elem-set;
      merge-bag, diff-bag : bag × bag → bag
definitions
  types $bag = elem \xrightarrow{m} \mathbb{N}_1$
  functions
    empty-bag : ( ) → bag
    empty-bag( ) ≜ { };
    num-bag : elem × bag → $\mathbb{N}$
    num-bag(e, m) ≜ **if** e ∈ **dom** m **then** m(e) **else** 0;
    plus-bag : elem × bag → bag
    plus-bag(e, m) ≜ m † {e ↦ num-bag(e,m) + 1};
    mems-bag : bag → elem-set
    mems-bag(m) ≜ **dom** m;
    merge-bag : bag × bag → bag
    merge-bag(m-1,m-2) ≜ {e ↦ num-bag(e,m-1)+
        num-bag(e,m-2) | e ∈ **dom** m-1 ∪ **dom** m-2};
    diff-bag : bag × bag → bag
    diff-bag(m-1,m-2) ≜ {e ↦ num-bag(e,m-1) –
        num-bag(e,m-1)|(e ∈ **dom** m-1) ∧
        (num-bag(e,m-1)>num-bag(e,m-2))}
end Multiset

To use these functions, the module *Multiset* must be instantiated:

instantiation
  Cash **as** Multiset(elem → Coin)
    types bag
    functions
      empty-bag: ( ) → bag;
      num-bag : elem × bag → $\mathbb{N}$;
      plus-bag : elem × bag → bag;
      mems-bag : bag → elem-set;
      merge-bag, diff-bag : bag × bag → bag

10.3 Modules – Parameterized modules

and similarly for *Stock*, with *Ingredient* instead of *Coin*. The types *Cash* and *Stock* now become *Cash`bag* and *Stock`bag* respectively, and the expressions can be written by using the instantiated functions. For example the postcondition of *INSERT-COIN* becomes

$$TAKINGS = Cash`plus\text{-}bag(new\text{-}coin, TAKINGS^{\leftarrow})$$

As an illustration of the use of the state in a parameterized module, consider a prioritized queue. Entries (for example messages) arrive in any order, and are extracted according to their priority, highest priority first; within one priority the choice is arbitrary. As the same entry can arrive more than once, multisets are used.

>   **module** *P-queue*
>   **parameters**
>   **types** *Entry*
>   **functions**
>   *priority* : *Entry* → $\mathbb{N}$
>   **exports**
>   **operations**
>   *ENTER* : *Entry* $\xrightarrow{o}$ ( );
>   *EXTRACT* : ( ) $\xrightarrow{o}$ *Entry* | QUEUE-EMPTY
>   **instantiation**
>   *Entries* **as** *Multiset*(*elem* → *Entry*)
>   **types** *bag*
>   **functions**
>   *empty-bag* : ( ) → *bag*;
>   *num-bag* : *elem* × *bag* → $\mathbb{N}$;
>   *plus-bag* : *elem* × *bag* → *bag*;
>   *mems-bag* : *bag* → *elem*-**set**;
>   *merge-bag*, *diff-bag* : *bag* × *bag* → *bag*
>   **definitions**
>   **state** *P-queue* **of**
>   *QUEUE* : *Entries`bag*
>   **init** *mk-P-queue*(*q*) $\underline{\triangle}$ *q* = *Entries`empty-bag*
>   **end**
>   **operations**
>   *ENTER*(*e* : *Entry*)
>   **ext wr** *QUEUE*
>   **post** *QUEUE* = *Entries`plus-bag*(*e*, *QUEUE*$^{\leftarrow}$);

10.3 Modules – Parameterized modules

```
EXTRACT( ) e : Entry | QUEUE-EMPTY
    ext wr QUEUE
    post
        if QUEUE = Entries`empty-bag then
            e = QUEUE-EMPTY ∧ QUEUE = QUEUE⁻
        else
            (e ∈ Entries`mems-bag(QUEUE)) ∧
            (∀ e' ∈ Entries`mems-bag(QUEUE) ·
                priority(e) ≥ priority(e')) ∧
            (QUEUE = Entries`diff-bag(e, QUEUE⁻))
end P-queue
```

The module *Clearing-house* uses this module to set up and manipulate a set of prioritized queues of messages, based on their destinations:

```
module Clearing-house
    instantiation
        Msg-queue as P-queue (Entry → Message, priority →
            Message-priority)
        operations
            ENTER : Entry ⇢ ( );
            EXTRACT: ( ) ⇢ Entry | QUEUE-EMPTY
    Entries as Multiset(elem → Entry)
        types bag
        functions
            empty-bag: : ( ) → bag;
            num-bag : elem × bag → ℕ;
            plus-bag : elem × bag → bag;
            mems-bag : bag → elem-set;
            merge-bag, diff-bag : bag × bag → bag
    exports
        types Message, Destination
        functions Message-priority : Message → ℕ
        operations
            ENTER : Message ⇢ ( );
            EXTRACT: Destination ⇢ Message | QUEUE-EMPTY
```

177

10.3 Modules – Parameterized modules

definitions
  types
    Destination = CAMBRIDGE | LEICESTER | MANCHESTER;
    Message :: PRIORITY : $\mathbb{N}$
              DEST   : *Destination*
              TEXT   : **char***
  state *Clearing-house* **of**
    QUEUES : *Destination* $\xrightarrow{m}$ *Msg-bags* ` *Bag*
    init *mk-Clearing-house*(q) $\triangleq$ q = { }
  end
  operations
    ENTER : *Message* $\rightarrow$ ( )
    ENTER (m) $\triangleq$
      Msg-queue ` ENTER(m) **using** QUEUES(m.DEST);

    EXTRACT(d : *Destination*) m : *Message* | QUEUE-EMPTY
      ext wr QUEUES : *Destination* $\xrightarrow{m}$ *Msg-bags* ` *Bag*
      post *Msg-queue* ` post-EXTRACT(QUEUES(d),
        QUEUES$^{\leftarrow}$(d), m)
end *Clearing-house*

10.4 Names

10.4.1 Syntax

   name = {identifier, '`'}, simple name;

   simple name = identifier | old name;

   name list = name, {',', name};

10.4.2 Meaning

Names are generalizations of identifiers, to allow reference to entities across modules. A name is an identifier preceded by a sequence of module identifiers separated by grave accents:

   Id, $Id_1\ `Id$,   $Id_2\ `Id_1\ `Id$,   $Id_3\ `Id_2\ `Id_1\ `Id$

Here Id is the local name of the entity, Id_1 is the identifier of the module from which the entity is originally imported; Id_2 is the module from which it is exported after being imported from Id_1, and so on. Any of the modules can be an ordinary module or an instantiation (see section 10.3).

For old names see section 8.2.

10.4.3 Examples

See section 10.3.3.

Appendix A Collected Mathematical Syntax

A.1 Introduction

This is the complete definition of the mathematical syntax in alphabetical order of construct name, with the section numbers in this book where the constructs are defined added as comments.

The following is a description of the syntactic metalanguage used in the VDM-SL standard and this book. It is taken from BS 6154:1981 (Method of defining syntactic metalanguage), but has been changed slightly to remove certain unused features. Many of the syntax rules include a comment to explain their meaning; inside a comment a meta identifier is enclosed in angle brackets < and > to avoid confusion with similar English words. The non-terminal symbols <letter>, <decimal digit>, and <character> are not defined. The position of <comments> is stated in a comment but not formally defined.

syntax = syntax rule, {syntax rule};

syntax rule = meta identifier, '=', definitions list, ';'
(* A <syntax rule> defines the sequences of symbols represented by a <meta identifier>. *);

definitions list = single definition, {'|', single definition}
(* | separates alternative <single definitions>. *);

single definition = term, {',', term}
(* , separates successive <terms>. *);

term = primary, ['–', exception]
(* A <term> represents any sequence of symbols that is defined by the <primary> but is not defined by the <exception>. *);

exception = primary
(* A <primary> may be used as an <exception> if it could be replaced by a <primary> containing no <meta identifiers>. *);

181

Appendix A Collected Mathematical Syntax

primary = optional sequence | repeated sequence | grouped sequence
| meta identifier | terminal string | empty;

optional sequence = '[', definitions list, ']'
(* The brackets [and] enclose symbols which are optional. *);

repeated sequence = '{', definitions list, '}'
(* The brackets { and } enclose symbols which may be repeated any number of times. *);

grouped sequence = '(', definitions list, ')'
(* The brackets (and) allow any <definitions list> to be a <primary>. *)

meta identifier = letter, {letter | decimal digit}
(* A <meta identifier> is the name of a syntactic element of the language being defined. *);

terminal string = " ' ", character - " ' ", {character - " ' "}, " ' "
| ' " ', character - ' " ', {character - ' " '}, ' " '
(* A <terminal string> represents the <characters> between the quote symbols ' ' or " ". *);

empty = ;

comment = '(*', {comment symbol}, '*)'
(* A comment is allowed anywhere outside a <terminal string> or <meta identifier>. *);

comment symbol = terminal string | character;

A.2   VDM-SL Mathematical Syntax

always handler = **'always'**, statement;   (*9.3*)

application = map application | sequence application
| function application;   (*6.1*)

arithmetic infix operator = '+' | '−' | '×' | '/' | '↑' | **'rem'** | **'mod'** | **'div'**
| '<' | '≤' | '>' | '≥';   (*4.3*)

arithmetic prefix operator = '+' | '−' | **'abs'** | **'floor'**;   (*4.3*)

assign command = state designator, ':=', expression
| state designator, ':=', operation call;   (*9.4*)

182

Appendix A Collected Mathematical Syntax

```
basic type expression = 'B' | 'N' | 'N₁' | 'Z' | 'Q' | 'R' | 'char'
   | 'token';                                                    (*4.1*)
basic type membership identifier= 'is-', ('B' | 'N' | 'N₁' | 'Z' | 'Q'
   | 'R' | 'char' | 'token');                                    (*2.3*)
binary expression = expression, infix operator, expression;      (*6.3*)
bind = set bind | type bind;                                     (*6.2*)
bind list = bind list item, {',', bind list item};               (*6.2*)
bind list item = pattern list, 'ε', expression
   | pattern list, ':', type expression;                         (*6.2*)
bind preamble = declaration preamble | definition preamble
   | let preamble | let be preamble;                             (*9.2*)
block statement = '(', single statement, {';', command}, ')';    (*9.2*)
boolean literal = 'true' | 'false';                          (*2.3, 4.2*)
bracketed expression = '(', expression, ')';                     (*6.1*)
bracketed type expression = '(', type expression, ')';           (*3.2*)
cases command = 'cases', expression, ':', command choice list,
   [',', others command choice], 'end';                          (*9.7*)
cases expression = 'cases', expression, ':', expression choice list,
   [',', others expression choice], 'end';                       (*6.5*)
character = letter | digit | delimiter character | other character
   | separator;                                                  (*2.2*)
character literal = " ' ", character - separator, " ' ";     (*2.3, 4.4*)
command = block command | assign command | nondeterministic command
   | sequence loop | set loop | indexed loop | while loop | call command
   | McCarthy command | if command | cases command | return command
   | exit command | error command | identity command;            (*9.2*)
command choice = pattern list, '→', statement;                   (*9.7*)
command choice list = command choice, {',', command choice};     (*9.7*)
comment = '--', {character - newline}, newline;                  (*2.4*)
complex expression = definition expression | let expression
   | let be expression;                                          (*6.4*)
composite expression = if expression | cases expression;         (*6.5*)
```

183

Appendix A Collected Mathematical Syntax

composite type expression = **'compose'**, identifier, **'of'**, field list,
   'end'; (*5.5*)

declaration item = identifier, ':', type expression, [':=', expression]
  | identifier, ':', type expression, [':=', operation call]; (*9.2*)

declaration preamble = **'dcl'**, declaration item, ';'; (*9.2*)

definition block = type definition block | state definition
  | value definition block | function definition block
  | operation definition block; (*3.1, 10.1*)

definition block list = definition block, {',', definition block};
  (*3.1, 10.1*)

definition expression = **'def'**, pattern or bind, '=', expression,
  {',', pattern or bind, '=', expression}, **'in'**, expression; (*6.4*)

definition item = pattern or bind, '=', expression
  | pattern or bind, '=', operation call; (*9.2*)

definition part = **'definitions'**, definition block list; (*10.1*)

definition preamble = **'def'**, definition item, {';', definition item};
  (*9.2*)

delimiter = keyword | delimiter character | compound delimiter;
  (*2.3*)

discretionary type expression = type expression | '(', ')'; (*5.8, 8.3*)

document = module list | definition block list; (*3.1, 10.1*)

dont care = '-'; (*6.2*)

elseif command clause = **'elseif'**, expression, **'then'**, statement;
  (*9.7*)

elseif expression clause = **'elseif'**, expression, **'then'**, expression;
  (*6.5*)

error command = **'error'**; (*9.2*)

error definition = identifier, ':', expression, '→', expression; (*8.2*)

error definition block = **'errs'**, error definition, {error definition};
  (*8.2*)

existential quantified expression = '∃', bind list, '·', expression;
  (*6.6*)

exit command = **'exit'**, [expression]; (*9.3*)

184

Appendix A Collected Mathematical Syntax

explicit function definition = identifier, ':', function type expression,
   identifier, parameter clause list ('$\underline{\triangle}$', expression,
   ['**pre**', expression] | '**is**' '**not**' '**yet**' '**defined**');   (*7.3*)

explicit operation definition = identifier, ':', operation type expression,
   identifier, parameter clause, [external variable clause],
   ('$\underline{\triangle}$', statement, ['**pre**', expression] | '**is**' '**not**' '**yet**' '**defined**');
                                                                                 (*8.3*)

exponent = '$\times 10 \uparrow$', ['+' | '−'], numeral;   (*2.3, 4.3*)

expression = unary expression | binary expression | complex expression
   | composite expression | quantified expression | iota expression
   | bracketed expression | application | function instantiation
   | field selection | lambda expression | type membership expression
   | undefined expression | symbolic literal | name | set expression
   | sequence expression | map expression | record expression
   | tuple expression;   (*6.1*)

expression choice = pattern list, '→', expression;   (*6.5*)

expression choice list = expression choice, {',', expression choice};   (*6.5*)

expression list = expression, {',', expression};   (*5.4, 6.1*)

external variable clause = '**ext**', external variable item,
   {external variable item};   (*8.2*)

external variable item = mode, name list, [':', type expression];   (*8.2*)

field = [identifier, ':'], type expression;   (*5.5*)

field list = {field};   (*5.5*)

field reference = state designator, '.', identifier;   (*9.4*)

field selection = expression, '.', identifier;   (*5.5*)

function application = expression, '(', [expression list], ')';   (*5.8*)

function definition = implicit function definition;
   | explicit function definition;   (*7.1*)

function definition block = '**functions**', function definition,
   {';', function definition};   (*7.1*)

function infix operator = '↑' | '∘';   (*5.8*)

function instantiation = expression, '[', type expression,
   {',', type expression}, ']';   (*7.5*)

Appendix A Collected Mathematical Syntax

function signature = name list, ':', function type expression; (*10.1*)

function signature block = **'functions'**, function signature,
  {';', function signature}; (*10.1*)

function type expression = discretionary type expression, '→',
  type expression; (*5.8*)

general infix operator = '=' | '≠'; (*6.3*)

general map type expression = type expression, '$\xrightarrow{m}$', type expression; (*5.3*)

general sequence type expression = type expression, '*'; (*5.4*)

guarded statement list = expression, '→', statement,
  {',', expression, '→', statement}; (*9.7*)

handler = always handler | nonrecursive handler
  | recursive handler; (*9.3*)

identifier = (plain letter | Greek letter),
  {plain letter | Greek letter | digit | " ' "| '-'}; (*2.3*)

identity command = **'skip'**; (*9.2*)

if command = **'if'**, expression, **'then'**, statement,
  {elseif command clause}, **'else'**, statement; (*9.7*)

if expression = **'if'**, expression, **'then'**, expression,
  {elseif expression clause}, **'else'**, expression; (*6.5*)

implicit function definition = identifier, typed parameter clause,
  typed identifier, (['**pre**', expression], '**post**', expression
  | '**is**', '**not**', '**yet**', '**defined**'); (*7.2*)

implicit operation definition = identifier, typed parameter clause,
  [typed identifier], [external variable clause],
  (['**pre**', expression], '**post**', expression, [error definition block]
  | '**is**', '**not**', '**yet**', '**defined**'); (*8.2*)

import definition = **'from'**, identifier, module signature; (*10.2*)

indexed loop = **'for'**, identifier, '=', expression, **'to'**,
  expression, ['**by**', expression], '**do**', statement; (*9.6*)

infix operator = general infix operator | logical infix operator
  | arithmetic infix operator | set infix operator
  | sequence infix operator | map infix operator
  | function infix operator; (*6.3*)

initialization definition = '**init**', pattern, '$\triangle$', expression; (*3.4*)

Appendix A Collected Mathematical Syntax

injective map type expression = type expression, '$\stackrel{m}{\leftrightarrow}$', type expression;
(*5.3*)

interface part = [module parameter section], [module import section], [module instantiation section], [module export section];   (*10.1*)

invariant definition = '**inv**', pattern, '$\underline{\triangle}$', expression;   (*3.2, 3.4*)

iota expression = 'ι', bind, '$\cdot$', expression;   (*6.6*)

lambda expression = 'λ', type bind list, '$\cdot$', expression;   (*5.8*)

let be expression = '**let**', bind, ['**be**', '**st**', expression], '**in**', expression;   (*6.4*)

let be preamble = '**let**', bind, ['**be**', '**st**', expression], '**in**';   (*9.2*)

let expression = '**let**', pattern or bind, '=', expression, {',', pattern or bind, '=', expression}, '**in**', expression;   (*6.4*)

let preamble = '**let**', pattern or bind, '=', expression, {',', pattern or bind, '=', expression}, '**in**';   (*9.2*)

letter = plain letter | keyword letter | distinguished letter | Greek letter;   (*2.2*)

logical infix operator = '$\wedge$' | '$\vee$' | '$\Rightarrow$' | '$\Leftrightarrow$';   (*4.2*)

logical prefix operator = '$\neg$';   (*4.2*)

map application = expression, '(', expression, ')';   (*5.3*)

map comprehension = '{', maplet, '|', bind list, ['$\cdot$', expression], '}';
(*5.3*)

map enumeration = '{', maplet, {',', maplet}, '}' | '{', '$\mapsto$', '}';   (*5.3*)

map expression = map enumeration | map comprehension;   (*5.3*)

map infix operator = '$\cup$' | '$\dagger$' | '$\triangleleft$' | '$\blacktriangleleft$' | '$\triangleright$' | '$\blacktriangleright$' | '$\uparrow$' | '$\circ$';   (*5.3*)

map postfix operator = '$^{-1}$';   (*5.3*)

map prefix operator = '**dom**' | '**rng**' | '**merge**';   (*5.3*)

map reference = state designator, '(', expression, ')';   (*9.4*)

map type expression = general map type expression | injective map type expression;   (*5.3*)

maplet = expression, '$\mapsto$', expression;   (*5.3*)

match value = '(', expression, ')';   (*6.2*)

Appendix A Collected Mathematical Syntax

McCarthy command = '(', guarded statement list,
   [',', others command choice], ')'; (*9.7*)

mode = **'rd'** | **'wr'**; (*8.2*)

module = **'module'**, identifier, interface part,
   [definition part], **'end'**, identifier; (*10.1*)

module export section = **'exports'**, module signature; (*10.2*)

module import section = **'imports'**, import definition,
   {',', import definition}; (*10.2*)

module instance = identifier, '(', [substitution, {',', substitution}], ')',
   [module signature]; (*10.3*)

module instantiation = identifier, **'as'**, module instance; (*10.3*)

module instantiation section = **'instantiation'**, module instantiation,
   {',', module instantiation}; (*10.3*)

module list = module, {module}; (*10.1*)

module parameter section = **'parameters'**, module signature; (*10.3*)

module signature = signature block, {signature block}; (*10.1*)

name = {identifier, '"'}, simple name; (*10.4*)

name list = name, {',', name}; (*10.4*)

nil literal = **'nil'**; (*2.3, 5.7*)

nondeterministic command = '||', '(', statement, {',', statement}, ')';
  (*9.5*)

nonempty sequence type expression = type expression, '$^+$'; (*5.4*)

nonrecursive handler = **'trap'**, pattern or bind, **'with'**, statement;
  (*9.3*)

numeral = digit, {digit}; (*2.3, 4.3*)

numeric literal = numeral, ['.', digit, {digit}], [exponent]; (*2.3, 4.3*)

old name = identifier, '$\leftarrow$'; (*8.2*)

operation call = name, '(', [expression list], ')',
   [**'using'**, state designator]; (*8.4*)

operation definition = implicit operation definition;
   | explicit operation definition; (*8.1*)

Appendix A Collected Mathematical Syntax

operation definition block = '**operations**', operation definition,
   {';', operation definition};   (*8.1*)

operation signature = name list, ':', operation type expression,
   ['**using**', name];   (*10.1*)

operation signature block = '**operations**', operation signature,
   {';', operation signature};   (*10.1*)

operation type expression = discretionary type expression, '$\xrightarrow{o}$',
   discretionary type expression;   (*8.3*)

optional type expression = '[', type expression, ']';   (*5.7*)

others command choice = '**others**', '→', statement;   (*9.7*)

others expression choice = '**others**', '→', expression;   (*6.5*)

parameter clause = '(', [pattern list], ')';   (*7.3*)

parameter clause list = parameter clause, {parameter clause};   (*7.3*)

pattern = pattern identifier | dont care | match value | set pattern
   | sequence pattern | tuple pattern | record pattern;   (*6.2*)

pattern identifier = identifier;   (*6.2*)

pattern list = pattern, {',', pattern};   (*6.2*)

pattern or bind = pattern | bind;   (*6.2*)

polymorphic function definition =
   identifier, type variable list, ':', function type expression,
   identifier, parameter clause list, ('$\triangle$', expression,
   ['**pre**', expression] | '**is**', '**not**', '**yet**', '**defined**');   (*7.5*)

postfix expression = expression, postfix operator;   (*6.3*)

postfix operator = map postfix operator;   (*6.3*)

prefix expression = prefix operator, expression;   (*6.3*)

prefix operator = logical prefix operator | arithmetic prefix operator
   | set prefix operator | sequence prefix operator
   | map prefix operator;   (*6.3*)

product type expression = type expression, '×', type expression;
      (*5.6*)

quantified expression = universal quantified expression
   | existential quantified expression | unique quantified expression;
      (*6.6*)

Appendix A Collected Mathematical Syntax

quote literal = distinguished letter, {'-' | distinguished letter};
$\qquad\qquad\qquad\qquad\qquad\qquad\qquad\qquad\qquad\qquad$ (*2.3, 4.5*)

quote type expression = quote literal; (*4.1, 4.5*)

record construction = identifier, '(', expression list, ')'; (*5.5*)

record expression = record construction | record modification; (*5.5*)

record modification = 'μ', '(', expression, ',', record modifier,
{',', record modifier}, ')'; (*5.5*)

record modifier = identifier, '↦', expression; (*5.5*)

record pattern = name, '(', pattern list, ')'; (*6.2*)

recursive handler = 'tixe', trap definition list; (*9.3*)

return command = 'return', [expression]; (*9.3*)

separator = space | newline; (*2.2*)

sequence application = expression, '(', expression, ')'; (*5.4*)

sequence comprehension = '[', expression, '|', set bind,
['·', expression], ']'; (*5.4*)

sequence concatenation pattern = pattern, '⌢', pattern; (*6.2*)

sequence enumeration = '[', [expression list], ']'; (*5.4*)

sequence enumeration pattern = '[', pattern list, ']'; (*6.2*)

sequence expression = sequence enumeration | sequence comprehension
| subsequence expression | sequence modification; (*5.4*)

sequence infix operator = '⌢'; (*5.4*)

sequence loop = 'for', pattern, 'in', ['reverse'], expression,
'do', statement; (*9.6*)

sequence modification = expression, '†', '{', sequence modifier,
{',', sequence modifier}, '}'; (*5.4*)

sequence modifier = expression, '↦', expression; (*5.4*)

sequence pattern = sequence enumeration pattern
| sequence concatenation pattern; (*6.2*)

sequence prefix operator = 'hd' | 'tl' | 'len' | 'elems' | 'inds' | 'conc';
$\qquad\qquad\qquad\qquad\qquad\qquad\qquad\qquad\qquad\qquad$ (*5.4*)

sequence reference = state designator, '(', expression, ')'; (*9.4*)

Appendix A Collected Mathematical Syntax

```
sequence type expression = general sequence type expression
    | nonempty sequence type expression;                    (*5.4*)
set bind = pattern, '∈', expression;                        (*6.2*)
set comprehension = '{', expression, '|', bind list, ['·', expression], '}';
                                                            (*5.2*)
set enumeration = '{', [expression list], '}';              (*5.2*)
set enumeration pattern = '{', pattern list, '}';           (*6.2*)
set expression = set enumeration | set comprehension
    | set range expression;                                 (*5.2*)
set infix operator = '∪' | '∩' | '-' | '⊆' | '⊂' | '∈' | '∉';  (*5.2*)
set loop =
    'for', 'all', pattern, '∈', expression, 'do', statement; (*9.6*)
set pattern = set enumeration pattern | set union pattern;  (*6.2*)
set prefix operator = 'card' | '𝓕' | '⋃' | '⋂';             (*5.2*)
set range expression = '{', expression, ',', '...', ',', expression, '}';
                                                            (*5.2*)
set type expression = type expression, '-set';              (*5.2*)
set union pattern = pattern, '∪', pattern                   (*6.2*)
signature block = type signature block | value signature block
    | function signature block | operation signature block; (*10.1*)
simple name = identifier | old name;                        (*10.4*)
single statement = [handler, 'in'], {bind preamble},
    command;                                                (*9.2*)
state definition = 'state', identifier, 'of', field list,
    [invariant definition], [initialization definition], 'end';  (*3.4*)
state designator = name | field reference | map reference
    | sequence reference;                                   (*9.4*)
statement = single statement | block statement;             (*9.2*)
subsequence expression = expression, '(', expression, ',', '...', ',',
    expression, ')';                                        (*5.4*)
substitution = identifier, '→', name;                       (*10.3*)
symbol = delimiter | identifier | type variable identifier
    | basic type membership identifier | symbolic literal;  (*2.3*)
```

Appendix A Collected Mathematical Syntax

symbolic literal = boolean literal | numeric literal | character literal
| text literal | quote literal | nil literal; (*2.3*)

text literal = ' " ', {' "" ' | character – (' " ' | separator)}, ' " ';
 (*2.3, 4.4*)

trap definition list = '{', pattern or bind, '↦', statement,
 {pattern or bind, '↦', statement}, '}'; (*9.3*)

tuple construction = 'mk-', '(', expression list, ')'; (*5.6*)

tuple expression = tuple construction; (*5.6*)

tuple pattern = 'mk-', '(', pattern list, ')'; (*6.2*)

type bind = pattern, ':', type expression; (*6.2*)

type bind list = type bind, {',', type bind}; (*6.2*)

type definition = identifier, '=', type expression, [invariant definition]
 | identifier, '::', field list, [invariant definition]
 | identifier, **'is'**, **'not'**, **'yet'**, **'defined'**; (*3.2*)

type definition block = **'types'**, type definition, {';', type definition};
 (*3.2*)

type description = name | type definition; (*10.1*)

type expression = bracketed type expression | type name
 | basic type expression | quote type expression
 | composite type expression | union type expression
 | set type expression | sequence type expression | map type expression
 | function type expression | optional type expression
 | product type expression | type variable; (*3.2*)

type membership expression = identifier, '(', expression, ')'
 | basic type membership identifier, '(', expression, ')'; (*3.2*)

type name = name; (*3.2*)

type signature block = **'types'**, type description, {';', type description};
 (*10.1*)

type variable = type variable identifier; (*3.2*)

type variable identifier = '@', identifier; (*2.3, 7.5*)

type variable list = '[', type variable identifier,
 {',', type variable identifier}, ']'; (*7.5*)

typed identifier = identifier, ':', type expression; (*7.2*)

typed parameter clause = '(', [typed pattern list], ')'; (*7.2*)

Appendix A Collected Mathematical Syntax

typed pattern list = pattern list, ':', type expression,
   {',', pattern list, ':', type expression}; (*7.2*)

unary expression = prefix expression | postfix expression; (*6.3*)

undefined expression = **'undefined'**; (*6.1, 7.3*)

union type expression = type expression, '|', type expression; (*5.7*)

unique quantified expression = '∃!', bind, '·', expression; (*6.6*)

universal quantified expression = '∀' bind list, '·', expression; (*6.6*)

value definition = pattern, [':', type expression], '=', expression,
   | pattern [':', type expression], **'is'**, **'not'**, **'yet'**, **'defined'**; (*3.3*)

value definition block = **'values'**, value definition,
   {';', value definition}; (*3.3*)

value description = name list, ':', type expression; (*10.1*)

value signature block = **'values'**, value description,
   {';', value description}; (*10.1*)

while loop = **'while'**, expression, **'do'**, statement; (*9.6*)

Appendix B ISO 646 Syntax

B.1 General

The character set consists of the following subset of the coded character set defined in ISO 646-1983 (ISO 7-bit coded character set for information interchange); see Table 1.

- The format effectors horizontal tabulation, line feed, vertical tabulation, form feed, and carriage return (0/9 to 0/13).

- The character space (2/0).

- All the graphic characters (2/1 to 7/14), with allocations from BS 4730:1985 (UK 7-bit coded character set) for the alternative or unallocated combinations.

The characters # and $ have alternatives £ (pound sign) and ¤ (currency sign) respectively. The national characters which ISO 646 allows to replace the characters [, \,], ^, `, {, |, }, and ~, are not allowed.

The symbols and separators are defined as follows.

B.2 Keywords and identifiers

Keywords are represented by transliterating the keyword letters **a** to **z** into the corresponding small letters a to z.

In identifiers, plain letters and digits are represented by the same characters. Greek letters are represented by the number sign # followed by the corresponding letter as shown below.

α	β	γ	δ	ε	ζ	η	θ	ι	κ	λ	μ	ν	ξ	ο	π	ρ	σ	τ	υ	φ	χ	ψ	ω
a	b	g	d	e	z	h	q	i	k	l	m	n	x	o	p	r	s	t	u	f	c	y	w
Α	Β	Γ	Δ	Ε	Ζ	Η	Θ	Ι	Κ	Λ	Μ	Ν	Ξ	Ο	Π	Ρ	Σ	Τ	Υ	Φ	Χ	Ψ	Ω
A	B	G	D	E	Z	H	Q	I	K	L	M	N	X	O	P	R	S	T	U	F	C	Y	W

Appendix B ISO 646 Syntax

The other characters used in forming identifiers are represented as follows: prime by the grave accent `, and hyphen by the underline _. The same character @ is used in type variable identifiers.

If an identifier coincides with a keyword, either one from the mathematical syntax transliterated as described below or one introduced in the ISO 646 syntax (see Table 26), then it is represented as above, preceded by the dollar sign $. This is to be avoided if possible, but it may be necessary, for example in transliterating from the mathematical syntax.

Examples of keywords and identifiers:

mathematical syntax	ISO 646 syntax
types	types
Vending-Machine-1	Vending_Machine_1
α''	#a``
return	$return

B.3   Literals

In a quote literal, the distinguished letters A to Z are represented by the corresponding capital letters A to Z, the whole quote literal being surrounded by < >.

In a numeric literal, the digits 0 to 9 are represented by the same characters; the decimal point is represented by the full stop '.', and the exponent sign $\times 10\uparrow$ by the capital letter E.

In character and string literals, the character quote ' and the string quote " are represented by the same characters (called the apostrophe ' and the quotation mark " respectively). As with the mathematical syntax, within a string literal a quotation mark is represented by two consecutive quotation marks "". Character literals are limited to graphic characters represented by single characters of the ISO 646 character set.

Examples of literals:

mathematical syntax	ISO 646 syntax
RED-AND-AMBER	<RED_AND_AMBER>
3.62 × 10 ↑ -2	3.62E-2
'X'	'X'
"A""string"""	"A""string"""

B.4 Separators and comments

The *space* separator is represented by any sequence of one or more space characters and/or horizontal tabulation characters, in any order. The *newline* separator is represented by one or more of the following character combinations: a carriage return character followed by a line feed, vertical tabulation, or form feed character, with or without any number of preceding and/or following space characters and horizontal tabulation characters.

A comment is as in the mathematical syntax: it runs from -- to the next carriage return. A particular method is provided in the ISO 646 syntax for annotations: an annotation runs from the keyword 'annotation' to the next occurrence of the keywords 'end annotation'. Annotations cannot be nested; any occurrence of 'annotation' within an annotation (or a comment) is ignored.

B.5 Delimiter characters and compound delimiters

Several ways are used to represent delimiter characters in the ISO 646 syntax. The ISO 646 equivalents for all delimiter characters are shown in Table 27.

- When the same character is available in the ISO 646 character set, that character is used.

- When the same character is not available in the ISO 646 character set, but a replacement character can be found, that replacement character is used.

- When the same character is not available in the ISO 646 character set, and no replacement character can be found, in some cases a sequence of characters is used.

Appendix B ISO 646 Syntax

- In other cases when the same character is not available in the ISO 646 character set, a new keyword or sequence of keywords (not used in the mathematical syntax) is used. This introduces new keywords, not in the mathematical syntax; the complete set of keywords for the ISO 646 syntax is shown in Table 26.

- In a handful of cases, for historical and sentimental reasons, a different order of symbols is used in the ISO 646.

B.6 Example Specification

Here is the example specification of section 1.3 transcribed into ISO 646 syntax.

```
types
    Drink = token     -- an unspecified type
    Money = nat       -- a whole number (of pence)

state Vending_Machine_1 of
    BALANCE : Money   -- money held by the machine during a transaction
    PRICES : map Drink to Money   -- the price of each type of drink
    inv mk_Vending_Machine_1(-, c) ==
        all c : Drink & c in set dom PRICES
        -- every drink always has a price; c stands for PRICES
    init mk_Vending_Machine_1(c, -) == c = 0
        -- initial state: no money in the machine; c stands for BALANCE

operations
    INSERT_MONEY(cash : Money)     -- customer inserts some money
    ext wr BALANCE : Money    -- this operation can alter the balance
    post BALANCE = BALANCE~ + cash
        -- the operation adds the money inserted to the balance

    GET_DRINK(choice : Drink) goods : Drink, change : Money
        -- customer chooses drink and gets drink and change
    ext    wr BALANCE : Money
           rd PRICES : map Drink to Money     -- this operation can alter
        -- the balance and read (but not alter) the price table
    pre BALANCE >= PRICES(choice)  -- the operation is defined only if
        -- the balance is enough to pay for the chosen drink
    post BALANCE = 0 and goods = choice
        and change = BALANCE~ - PRICES(choice)
        -- the effect is to clear the balance and to deliver the chosen drink
        -- and the change
```

Appendix B ISO 646 Syntax

Table 25   ISO 646 syntax: character set

	0	1	2	3	4	5	6	7
0	NUL	DLE	SP	0	@	P	`	p
1	SOH	DC1	!	1	A	Q	a	q
2	STX	DC2	"	2	B	R	b	r
3	ETX	DC3	#	3	C	S	c	s
4	EOT	DC4	$	4	D	T	d	t
5	ENQ	NAK	%	5	E	U	e	u
6	ACK	SYN	&	6	F	V	f	v
7	BEL	ETB	'	7	G	W	g	w
8	BS	CAN	(	8	H	X	h	x
9	HT	EM	)	9	I	Y	i	y
10	LF	SUB	*	:	J	Z	j	z
11	VT	ESC	+	;	K	[	k	{
12	FF	IS4	,	<	L	\	l	|
13	CR	IS3	-	=	M	]	m	}
14	SO	IS2	.	>	N	^	n	~
15	SI	IS1	/	?	O	_	o	DEL

Appendix B ISO 646 Syntax

Table 26 Keywords in the ISO 646 syntax

abs	all	always	and
annotation	as	be	bool
br	by	card	cases
char	compose	conc	dcl
def	defined	definitions	dinter
div	do	dom	dunion
elems	else	elseif	end
error	errs	exists	exists1
exit	exports	ext	false
floor	for	from	functions
hd	if	imports	in
inds	init	inmap	instantiation
int	inter	inv	inverse
iota	is	lambda	len
let	map	merge	mod
module	mu	nat	nat1
nil	not	of	operations
or	others	parameters	post
power	pre	psubset	rat
rb	rd	real	rem
return	reverse	rng	rt
seq	seq1	set	skip
st	state	subset	then
tixe	tl	to	token
tr	trap	true	types
undefined	union	using	values
while	with	wr	yet

Appendix B ISO 646 Syntax

Table 27 ISO 646 syntax summary

math.	ISO 646	math.	ISO 646	math.	ISO 646
,	,	$\wedge$	and	$\circ$	compose
:	:	$\vee$	or	$\frown$	conc
;	;	$\Rightarrow$	=>	ι	iota
.	.	$\Leftrightarrow$	<=>	λ	lambda
(	(	$\forall$	all	μ	mu
)	)	$\exists$	exists	$\mathcal{F}$	power
[	[	|	|	$\mathbb{B}$	bool
]	]	.	&	$\mathbb{N}$	nat
{	{	$\in$	in set	$\mathbb{N}_1$	nat1
}	}	$\notin$	not in set	$\mathbb{Z}$	int
+	+	$\cap$	inter	$\mathbb{Q}$	rat
$-$	$-$	$\cup$ (sets)	union	$\mathbb{R}$	real
$\times$	*	$\cup$ (maps)	merge	$\triangleq$	==
/	/	$\subset$	psubset	$\|\|$	||
$\uparrow$	**	$\subseteq$	subset	$\rightarrow$	->
=	=	$\bigcap$	dinter	$\xrightarrow{o}$	==>
$\neq$	<>	$\bigcup$	dunion	$\grave{}$	$\grave{}$
<	<	$\mapsto$	|->	$\dagger$	++
>	>	$\triangleright$	rt	::	::
$\leq$	<=	$\triangleleft$	tr	:=	:=
$\geq$	>=	$\triangleright\!\!\!\triangleright$	rb	...	...
$\neg$	not	$\triangleleft\!\!\!\triangleleft$	br	$\exists!$	exists1
				$\underleftarrow{}$	~
M^{-1}	inverse M	$T\text{-}\mathbf{set}$	set of T	T^*	seq of T
T^+	seq1 of T	$T \xrightarrow{m} T'$	map T to T'	$T \xleftrightarrow{m} T'$	inmap T to T'

201

Appendix C Examples of VDM-SL Specifications

C.1 Drinks vending machine, stage 2

This specification is a possible first refinement of the abstract vending machine specification of section 1.3.

The type Drink has been defined as tea, coffee, or chocolate, where tea and coffee can be taken with or without milk and sugar. The state has been enhanced to keep track of the stocks of ingredients and the takings. The operation of inserting money has been broken down into a sequence of operations for inserting individual coins, and the receipt of the drink and the change have been separated. An operation has been added to replenish the stocks and/or reset the price table. Two values have been added to give the value of each coin and the ingredients of each drink.

types
  Coin = ONE | TWO | FIVE | TEN | TWENTY | FIFTY;
  -- Decimalization has robbed us of more picturesque names for coins!
  Drink = *Tea-or-coffee* | CHOCOLATE;
  Tea-or-coffee :: *FLAVOUR* : TEA | COFFEE
                      WHITE : $\mathbb{B}$
                      SWEET : $\mathbb{B}$;
  Ingredient = TEA | COFFEE | CHOCOLATE | MILK | SUGAR | WATER;
  Money = $\mathbb{N}$;
  Prices = *Drink* $\xrightarrow{m}$ *Money*;
  Stock = *Ingredient* $\xrightarrow{m}$ $\mathbb{N}$
    inv $s \triangleq \forall i : Ingredient \cdot i \in$ **dom** s;
  Cash = *Coin* $\xrightarrow{m}$ $\mathbb{N}$
    inv $c \triangleq \forall co : Coin \cdot co \in$ **dom** c

Appendix C Examples of VDM-SL Specifications

values
   $WORTH: Coin \xrightarrow{m} Money \triangleq \{ONE \mapsto 1, TWO \mapsto 2, FIVE \mapsto 5,$
      $TEN \mapsto 10, TWENTY \mapsto 20, FIFTY \mapsto 50\};$
   $INGREDIENTS: Drink \xrightarrow{m} Ingredient\text{-set} \triangleq$
      $\{CHOCOLATE \mapsto \{CHOCOLATE, WATER\}\} \cup$
         $\{d \mapsto \{d.FLAVOUR, WATER\} \cup (\textbf{if } d.WHITE \textbf{ then } \{MILK\} \textbf{ else } \{\ \}) \cup$
         $(\textbf{if } d.SWEET \textbf{ then } \{SUGAR\} \textbf{ else } \{\ \}) \mid d: Tea\text{-}or\text{-}coffee\}$

state *Vending-Machine-2* **of**
   BALANCE : *Money*
   STOCKS : *Stock*
   CUPS : $\mathbb{N}$
   TAKINGS : *Cash*
   PRICES : *Prices*
   init $mk\text{-}Vending\text{-}Machine\text{-}1(B, S, C, T, P) \triangleq$
      $(B = 0)$
   $\wedge \ (S = \{i \mapsto 0 \mid i : Ingredient\})$
   $\wedge \ (C = 0)$
   $\wedge \ (T = \{c \mapsto 0 \mid c : Coin\})$
   $\wedge \ (P = \{d \mapsto 0 \mid d : Drink\})$
end

operations

   $SERVICE\ (new\text{-}stock: Stock, new\text{-}cups: \mathbb{N}, new\text{-}takings: Cash,$
      $new\text{-}prices: Prices)$
   ext wr *STOCKS* : *Stock*
      wr *CUPS* : $\mathbb{N}$
      wr *TAKINGS* : *Cash*
      wr *PRICES* : *Prices*
      rd *BALANCE* : *Money*
   pre $BALANCE = 0$
   post $(STOCK = new\text{-}stock)$
      $\wedge \ (CUPS = new\text{-}cups)$
      $\wedge \ (TAKINGS = new\text{-}takings)$
      $\wedge \ (PRICES = new\text{-}prices);$

Appendix C Examples of VDM-SL Specifications

INSERT-COIN(*cash* : *Money*)   -- customer inserts a coin
ext wr *BALANCE*: *Money*
       wr *TAKINGS* : *Cash*
post (*BALANCE* = *BALANCE*$^{\leftarrow}$ † *WORTH* (*new-coin*))

   ∧ (*TAKINGS* = *TAKINGS*$^{\leftarrow}$ †{*new-coin* ↦ *TAKINGS*$^{\leftarrow}$(*new-coin*)+1});

GET-DRINK(*choice* : *Drink*) *goods* : *Drink*
   -- customer chooses and gets drink
ext wr *BALANCE* : *Money*
       wr *STOCKS* : *Stock*
       wr *CUPS* : $\mathbb{N}$
       rd   *PRICES* : *Prices*
pre (∀ *i* ∈ *INGREDIENTS* (*choice*) · *STOCKS*(*i*) > 0)

   ∧ (*CUPS* > 0)

   ∧ (*BALANCE* ≥ *PRICES* (*choice*))
       -- the balance is enough to pay for the chosen drink
post (*BALANCE* = *BALANCE*$^{\leftarrow}$ – *PRICES*(*choice*))

   ∧ (*CUPS* = *CUPS*$^{\leftarrow}$ – 1)

   ∧ (*STOCKS* = *STOCKS*$^{\leftarrow}$ †

       {*i* ↦ *STOCKS*$^{\leftarrow}$(*i*) – 1 | *i* ∈ *INGREDIENTS*(*choice*)})

   ∧ (*goods* = *choice*);

GET-CHANGE( ) *change* : *Cash*
   -- customer gets change
ext wr *BALANCE* : *Money*
       wr *TAKINGS* : *Cash*
pre *makings*(*BALANCE*) ∩ *changes*(*TAKINGS*) ≠ { }
post (*BALANCE* = 0)

   ∧ (*change* ∈ *makings*(*BALANCE*$^{\leftarrow}$) ∩ *changes*(*TAKINGS*$^{\leftarrow}$))

   ∧ (∀ *c* : *Coin* · *num*(*change*, *c*) + *num*(*TAKINGS*,*c*) =
       num(*TAKINGS*$^{\leftarrow}$, *c*))

Appendix C Examples of VDM-SL Specifications

functions

$value : Cash \rightarrow Money$
$value(c) \triangleq sum(\{WORTH(co) \times c(co) \cdot co \in \mathbf{dom}\ c\});$
-- money value of cash sum c

$sum : \mathbb{N}_1\text{-}\mathbf{set} \rightarrow \mathbb{N}$
$sum(s) \triangleq \mathbf{if}\ s = \{\}\ \mathbf{then}\ 0$
    $\mathbf{else\ let}\ m \in s\ \mathbf{in}\ m + sum(s - \{m\});$
-- sum of elements of set s of positive integers

$makings : Money \rightarrow Cash\text{-}\mathbf{set}$
$makings(m) \triangleq \{c \mid c : Cash \cdot value(c) = m\};$
-- all possible ways of making up the sum of money m

$changes : Cash \rightarrow Cash\text{-}\mathbf{set}$
$changes(ch) \triangleq \{c \mid c : Cash \cdot (\mathbf{dom}\ c \subseteq \mathbf{dom}\ ch) \land$
    $\forall co \in \mathbf{dom}\ c \cdot c(co) \leq ch(co)\};$
-- all possible sums of money that can be returned as change from ch

$num : Cash \times Coin \rightarrow \mathbb{N}$
$num(c, co) \triangleq \mathbf{if}\ co \in \mathbf{dom}\ c\ \mathbf{then}\ c(co)\ \mathbf{else}\ 0;$
-- number of coins of denomination co in c

Appendix C Examples of VDM-SL Specifications

C.2   Reversi

This is a specification of the rules of the old English game of Reversi. The specification has 5 parts:

- types representing the playing equipment and players;

- state variables representing the state of play;

- an initialization to set up the initial state;

- a nondeterministic operation PLAY yielding the states arising from the given state by legal plays;

- an operation RESULT returning whether the game is over, and if so which player (if either) won.

For those unfamiliar with it, the rules of the game are as follows.

1 The game is between 2 players, Blue and Yellow, and is played on the squares of an 8x8 board with disc-shaped pieces, blue on one side and yellow on the other. Pieces blue side up are Blue's and pieces yellow side up are Yellow's. Initially the board is empty and each player has a stock of 32 pieces.

2 The players play alternately, except that a player who has no legal play on his turn misses that turn. To decide who plays first, one player tosses a piece and the other calls a colour; the winner of the toss has the choice of playing first or second.

3. For the first two plays by each player, a legal play by a player consists in placing a piece from his stock in a vacant one of the central 4 squares of the board, with his colour up. Thereafter, a legal play by a player consists in placing a piece from his stock in a vacant square, with his colour up, so that it traps (see below) at least one of his opponent's pieces on the board; and then turning over all his opponent's pieces that are trapped by the piece just placed (so that they become his).

A player A's piece X traps one of his opponent B's pieces Y on the board if Y lies between X and another of A's pieces Z, in a straight line orthogonally or diagonally, and all squares in line between X and Z are occupied by B's pieces.

Appendix C Examples of VDM-SL Specifications

4. A player cannot play if there are no pieces left in his stock, or if he cannot place a piece according to rule 3. The game ends when neither player can play; if the players have equal numbers of pieces on the board then the game is tied, otherwise the player with more pieces on the board wins.

The VDM model presented here simplifies the rules in 2 respects.

- In practice, the first 4 moves always give a position of the form $\begin{smallmatrix}BB\\YY\end{smallmatrix}$ in the centre, so this is taken as the starting position in the VDM model. (The other possibility $\begin{smallmatrix}BY\\YB\end{smallmatrix}$ is regarded as weak for the first player.)

- The rule for deciding who plays first is not modelled.

module *Reversi*
exports
  operations
    SET UP : ( ) $\xrightarrow{o}$ ( );
    PLAY   : ( ) $\xrightarrow{o}$ ( );
    RESULT : ( ) $\xrightarrow{o}$ $\mathbb{B}$ × [*Player*]
  types
    Player

definitions
  state *Reversi* **of**
    BOARD : *Position*
    TURN   : *Player*
    PIECES : *Stock*
  init *mk-Reversi*(*board*, *turn*, *pieces*) $\triangleq$
  let *init-board* $\triangleq$ {*mk-Square*(*x,y*) $\mapsto$ **if** *x* = 4 **then** *B* **else** *Y*
    | *x* ∈ {4,5} , *y* ∈ {4,5}} **in**
  (*board* = *init-board*)
  ∧ (*turn* = *B*)
  ∧ (*pieces* = {*B* $\mapsto$ 30, *Y* $\mapsto$ 30})

Appendix C Examples of VDM-SL Specifications

types
   Label = $\mathbb{Z}$-**set**
     inv $i \triangleq (i \geq 1) \wedge (i \leq 8)$;
   Square :: COL : *Label*
           ROW : *Label*;
   Player = $B \mid Y$;
   Position = *Square* $\xrightarrow{m}$ *Player*;
   Stock = *Player* $\xrightarrow{m}$ $\mathbb{N}$

operations

PLAY( )
   ext **wr** *BOARD* : *Position*
         wr *TURN* : *Player*
         wr *PIECES* : *Stock*
   pre *playable*(*BOARD*, *PIECES*)
   post
     def $pl \triangleq plays(BOARD^{\leftarrow}, TURN^{\leftarrow}, PIECES^{\leftarrow}(TURN^{\leftarrow}))$ **in**
     if $pl = \{\,\}$ **then**
        $(BOARD = BOARD^{\leftarrow}) \wedge (PIECES = PIECES^{\leftarrow})$
        -- player p misses his turn
     else
        $(\exists\, s \in pl \cdot BOARD = \{s \mapsto TURN^{\leftarrow}\} \cup \{t \mapsto$ **if** *captured*
          $(BOARD^{\leftarrow}, TURN^{\leftarrow}, s, t)$ **then** $TURN^{\leftarrow}$ **else** $BOARD^{\leftarrow}(t)$
          $\mid t \in$ **dom** $BOARD^{\leftarrow}\})$
        $\wedge (PIECES = PIECES^{\leftarrow} \dagger [TURN^{\leftarrow} \mapsto PIECES^{\leftarrow}(TURN^{\leftarrow})-1]))$
        $\wedge (TURN = oppo(TURN^{\leftarrow}))$;

RESULT : ( ) $\xrightarrow{o}$ $\mathbb{B} \times [Player]$
RESULT( )
   ext rd *BOARD* : *Position* $\triangle$
   if *playable*(*BOARD*, *PIECES*) **then** (false, nil)
   else let $b =$ **card** $\{s \mid (s \in$ **dom** $BOARD) \wedge (BOARD(s) = B)\}$ **in**
      let $y =$ **card** $\{s \mid (s \in$ **dom** $BOARD) \wedge (BOARD(s) = Y)\}$ **in**
      mk-(true, **if** $b > y$ **then** B **else if** $y > b$ **then** Y **else** nil)

Appendix C Examples of VDM-SL Specifications

functions

$playable : Position \times Stock \to \mathbb{B}$
-- at least one of the players can play in position b with stock c
$playable(b, c) \triangleq plays(b, B, c(B)) \cup plays(b, Y, c(Y)) \neq \{\ \}$;

$plays : Position \times Player \times \mathbb{Z} \to Square\text{-set}$
-- all squares where player p can play in position b with stock c
$plays(b,p,c) \triangleq$ **if** $c = 0$ **then** $\{\ \}$ **else**
  $\{s \mid s : Square \cdot (s \notin \textbf{dom } b) \wedge$
    $(\exists\, t \in Square \cdot captured(b,p,s,t))\}$

$captured : Position \times Player \times Square \times Square \to \mathbb{B}$
-- square t is captured by player p playing at square s in position b
$captured\,(b, p, s, t) \triangleq$
  $(\exists\, u \in \textbf{dom } b \cdot (b(u) = p) \wedge between(t,s,u)$
  $\wedge\ (\forall\, v : Square \cdot between(v,s,u)$
    $\Rightarrow$ **if** $v \in \textbf{dom } b$ **then** $b(v) = oppo(p)$ **else false**));

$between : Square \times Square \times Square \to \mathbb{B}$
-- square t is in line with and between squares s and u
$between(t,s,u) \triangleq (d(s,t) \times d(t,u) > 0)$
  $\wedge\ \exists\, k : \mathbb{Z} \cdot \exists\, i, j \in \{-1, 0, 1\} \cdot (((i \neq 0) \vee (j \neq 0))$
  $\wedge\ \forall\, v \in \{s,t,u\} \cdot i \times v.COL + j \times v.ROW = k)$;

$d : Square \times Square \to \mathbb{Z}$
-- signed 'distance' from square s to square t
$d(s,t) \triangleq$ **let** $x = t.COL - s.COL,\ y = t.ROW - s.ROW$ **in**
if $x \neq 0$ **then** x **else** y;

$oppo : Player \to Player$
-- player p's opponent
$oppo(p) \triangleq$ **if** $p = B$ **then** Y **else** B

end Reversi

Appendix C Examples of VDM-SL Specifications

The reader may like to prove the following theorems (invariant predicates on the state) by showing that they hold in the initial state and are preserved by the operations.

Theorem 1. The centre 4 squares are always occupied:

let $centre \triangleq \{mk\text{-}Square(x,y) | (x \in \{4,5\}) \wedge (y \in \{4,5\})\}$ **in**
  $centre \subseteq \textbf{dom } BOARD$

Theorem 2. The set of occupied squares is connected:

let $next : Square \times Square \rightarrow \mathbb{B} =$
  $\lambda u : Square, v : Square \cdot \textbf{abs } d(u,v)=1$ **in**
  let $conn : Square\text{-set} \rightarrow \mathbb{B} =$
    $\lambda q : Square\text{-set} \cdot \forall r, s \in q \cdot \exists t \in Square^+ \cdot (t(1)=r)$
    $\wedge \ (t(\textbf{len } t) = s)$
    $\wedge \ \forall \ i \in \textbf{inds tl } t \cdot (t(i) \in q) \wedge next(t(i),t(i-1))$ **in**
  $conn(\textbf{dom } BOARD)$

Theorem 3. At any time after the first play, there is a row of 3 adjacent pieces with the same colour up:

$BOARD = init\text{-}board \vee$
  $\exists \ s,t,u \in \textbf{dom } BOARD \cdot next(s,t) \wedge next(t,u) \wedge between(t,s,u)$
    $\wedge \ (BOARD(s)=BOARD(t)) \wedge (BOARD(t)=BOARD(u))$

Index

abnormal termination 143
abs 36
absolute value operator 36
abstract syntax 1
actual parameter 85, 141
addition operator 37
always 151
always handler 151
annotation 18
application 90
applicative expression 98
assign command 156
association 45, 98
basic type membership identifier 15, 30
basic type 6, 20, 29
be st 103, 148
binary expression 89, 97
bind 94
bind preamble 145, 146
binding 93
block statement 146
Boolean type 29, 31
bracketed expression 90
card 51
cardinality 51
cases 105, 165
cases command 165
cases expression 105
char 29, 42
character type 29, 42
character 12, 42
command 143, 145
comment 18
comparison operator 38
compatible maps 57
complex expression 90, 102
component of a tuple 78

compose 72
composite expression 90, 105
composite type expression 72
composite value 72
compound delimiter 15
compound type 20, 45
conc 67
concrete syntax 1
conditional command 164
conjunction operator 31
curried function 115, 124
dcl 146
decimal fraction 35
declaration 5
declaration preamble 146
def 102, 147
definition block list 19
definition block 19, 168
definition expression 102
definition part 168
definition preamble 147
definitions 168
delimiter character 12
delimiter 15
digit 12
disjoint union 94
disjunction operator 31
distinguished letter 44
distributed concatenation operator 67
distributed intersection operator 50
distributed merge operator 58
distributed union operator 50
div 37
division operator 37
document 19
dom 55
domain of a map 55
dont care 92, 93

213

Index

elements operator 68
elems 68
else 106, 164
elseif 106, 164
empty map 55
empty sequence 66
empty set 49
equality operator 32, 38, 50, 59, 68, 74, 79, 98
equivalence operator 32
error 146
error command 146
error condition 135
error definition block 134
error postcondition 135
error precondition 135
errs 135
existential quantified expression 109
exit 152
exit command 152
explicit function definition 121
explicit operation definition 139
exponent 36
exponentiation operator 37
exports 170
expression 89
ext 134
external variable clause 134
false 29, 31
field 25, 72
field reference 157
field selection 74, 90
finite subset operator 51
flat language 3, 19
flat type 45
flat value 45
floor 36
floor operator 36
for 160, 161
for all 160
function 2, 84, 115
function application 85
function composition operator 85
function definition 2, 115
function instantiation 90, 127

function iteration operator 86
function signature 169
function type 84
function type expression 84
generic module 173
global scope 5, 19
graph of a map 56
graphic character 12
greater than operator 38
greater than or equal to operator 38
handler 145, 151
hd 68
head operator 68
identifier 12, 14
identity operator 36
identity command 146
identity map 58
if 106, 164
if command 164
if expression 106
implementability 7
implication operator 32
implicit function definition 117
implicit operation definition 133
imports 170
inclusion operator 50
incomplete explicit function definition 122, 125
incomplete explicit operation definition 140
incomplete implicit function definition 120
incomplete implicit operation definition 137
incomplete polymorphic function definition 128
incomplete type definition 22
incomplete value definition 24
indexed loop 161
indices operator 68
inds 68
inequality operator 32, 38, 50, 59, 68, 74, 79, 98
infix operator 97
informal syntactic notation 8

Index

init 26
initialization definition 26
injective map 56
integer 29, 35
integer division operator 37
integer part operator 36
interface part 168
inv 21, 26
invariant 2, 6, 21
invariant definition 21, 26
inverse map operator 56
iota expression 90, 110
is not yet defined 22, 24, 120, 122, 125, 128, 137, 140
ISO 646 syntax 1, 195
keyword 12
lambda expression 86, 90
left association 98
len 68
length operator 68
less than operator 38
less than or equal to operator 38
let 102, 103, 147, 148
let be expression 103
let be preamble 148
let expression 102
let preamble 147
letter 12
lexical structure 11
logical operator 31
loop 160
loose specification 2, 118, 131
map 55
map application 59
map composition operator 58
map comprehension 57
map enumeration 56
map expression 91
map iteration operator 58
map merge operator 57
map override operator 58
map reference 157
map restriction operator 59
maplet arrow 56
match value 92, 93

matching 93
mathematical syntax 1
McCarthy command 165
membership operator 51
merge 57
minus operator 37
mod 37
mode 134
module 3, 19, 168
module 168
module export section 168, 170
module import section 168, 170
module instantiation section 168, 173
module list 19, 168
module parameter section 168, 173
module signature 168
modulus operator 37
multiplication operator 37
mutual recursion 121
name 91, 179
natural number 29, 35
negation operator 31, 36
newline 11
nil 81
nil literal 81
nil type 81
nil value 81
nondeterminism 3, 131
nondeterministic command 158
nonflat type 84
nonflat value 84
nonmembership operator 51
nonrecursive handler 151
normal termination 143
numeric literal 12, 35, 36
old name 134, 136
operation 2, 131
operation call 141
operation definition 2, 131
operation signature 169
operation type expression 131
operator association 98
operator precedence 97
optional type expression 81
ordering operator 38

Index

other character 12
others 105, 165
parameter 2, 115, 173
parameterized module 173
pattern 92
pattern identifier 92, 93
plus operator 37
polymorphic function definition 22, 127
polymorphic type expression 127
positive integer 29, 35
post 117, 133
postcondition 2, 117, 133
postfix operator 97
pre 118, 121, 134, 139
precedence 45, 97
precondition 118, 121, 134, 139
prefix operator 97
product type 78
proof obligation 7
proper inclusion operator 50
quantified expression 90, 109
quote literal 12, 44
quote type 30, 44
quote value 44
range of a map 55
rational number 29, 35
rd 134
real number type 29, 35
real number 29, 35
record 72
record construction 73
record expression 91
record modification 74
record pattern 94
recursion 21, 118, 121
recursive handler 152
rem 37
remainder operator 37
result 2, 115
return 152
return command 152
returned value 143
reverse 160
right association 98

rng 55
scope 5
separator 11, 12
sequence 65
sequence application 68
sequence comprehension 66
sequence concatenation operator 67
sequence concatenation pattern 94
sequence enumeration 66
sequence enumeration pattern 94
sequence expresion 91
sequence loop 160
sequence modification 67
sequence reference 157
sequence type 65
set 48
-**set** 48
set bind 94
set comprehension 49
set difference operator 50
set enumeration 48
set enumeration pattern 94
set expression 91
set intersection operator 50
set loop 160
set range expression 49
set type 48
set union operator 50
set union pattern 94
signature block 168
simple delimiter 15
single statement 146
skip 146
space 11
state 2, 25
state definition 25
state designator 156
state variable 25
statement 3, 145
strictness 20
subsequence 67
subsequence expression 67
subtraction operator 37
symbolic literal 15, 91
symbol 11

Index

tag 72
tail operator 68
text literal 42
text string 42
then 106, 164
times operator 37
tixe 152
tl 68
to the power of operator 37
token 30
token 30
token type 30
trap 151
true 29, 31
truth value 29, 31
tuple 78
tuple construction 79
tuple expression 91
tuple pattern 94
type 2, 20
type bind 95
type constructor 20, 45
type definition 2, 21
type description 169
type membership expression 22, 90
type variable 127
type variable identifier 14
unary expression 89, 97
unary minus operator 36
unary plus operator 36
undefined 91, 122
undefined expression 91, 122
undefined value 6, 20
underspecification 2, 118
union type expression 81
unique quantified expression 110
universal quantified expression 109
using 141
value definition 2, 24
value description 169
while 161
while loop 161
wr 134